THE
CAT LOVERS'
POCKET BIBLE

THE
CAT LOVERS'
POCKET BIBLE

CERYS OWEN

This edition first published in Great Britain 2009 by
Crimson Publishing, a division of Crimson Business Ltd
Westminster House
Kew Road
Richmond
Surrey
TW9 2ND

A catalogue record for this book is available from the British Library.

ISBN 978–1–907087–05–9

Typeset by RefineCatch Ltd, Bungay, Suffolk
Printed and bound by LegoPrint SpA, Trento

CONTENTS

INTRODUCTION

Have you ever wondered whether or not cats actually land on their feet when they fall? Why they supposedly have nine lives? Whether or not they really do like milk? Did you know that cats are the only domestic animal not mentioned in the Bible, that they are resident in every continent except Antarctica, and that Ernest Hemingway kept more than 30 in his house?

Cats have had a special relationship with man since ancient times, and from the worshiped feline goddesses of Egyptian times to Top Cat and Hello Kitty, they have always played a big part in human society and culture. Many believe that cats are man's *real* best friend, and their unique combination of independence and intelligence with an affectionate purry nature makes them both practical and irresistible pets.

The Cat Lovers' Pocket Bible entertains you with the history and trivia of cats. It also serves as an indispensable 'owner's manual' providing advice and tips on everything involved in owning a cat, from where to get your first moggy to dealing with pregnancy, vet visits, feeding time and, most importantly, playtime!

Whether you are already owned by a furry feline or are thinking about getting one, this is the book for you. Enjoyable at every level, the experts amongst you will be just as entertained as the novices by the plethora of funny facts and handy hints that lie within these pages, and as you take in the advice and information offered, you'll become a truly great owner.

As Jim Davis (of 'Garfield' fame) observantly noted, 'Way down deep, we're all motivated by the same urges. Cats have the courage to live by them.' This book is a celebration of everything that mischievous moggies embody, and indulges in every quirk and foible that has earned them the love and respect of humans for thousands of years. With the right care and attention, your independent furry friend will end up loving you just as much as you love her!

ABOUT CATS

✿ CAT FACTS ✿

There are a few specialised features that go into making cats cats.

EYES

- Cats have the largest eyes (in terms of relative size) of any mammal.

- They have superior vision at night, and they can see using one-sixth of the light we can.

- Cats' eyes contain a *tapetum lucidum* (a layer of tissue behind the retina) to improve their night vision and it is this tissue that causes the flashing or red eyes seen in pictures or in reflected light.

- Cats' pupils are an elliptical shape, meaning they can open and close much faster, therefore allowing more or less light in. This helps the cat hunt at night and explains the shape of big cats' eyes, which can often appear as slits.

- It has been argued, though, that cats are near-sighted and there is a common myth that cats can't see colour. In fact, cats respond to the purple, blue, green and yellow colour ranges. The colours red, orange and brown most likely appear as shades of grey to them.

- Cats are unable to see the area directly below their head, so make sure you don't put their food there!

EARS

- Cats' hearing, like their vision, is also superior to humans'. Their hearing range is around 65khz, whereas ours is 20khz, meaning cats are able to hear sounds we cannot hear.

- Cats are able to move their ears independently of each other, a trait which is often indicative of their mood; cats will lie their ears flat when angry but will turn them back when in a playful mood.

MOUTH

- Cats' tongues have special spines (a bit like hooks) which are used in both feeding and in their grooming. It is estimated that they spend 30% of their waking hours grooming.

- Cats are known for their hygiene and their cleaning habits. Cats' saliva contains a powerful cleaning agent but it is this agent which some people are allergic to.

- Due to a genetic fault which has been passed down through the ages, it is now widely believed that cats cannot taste sugary foods.

Purrfect

Cats are the only animals in the world to purr. They purr to show contentment, an instinctive trait which is used to stimulate milk from a mother cat feeding her kittens. Cats purr at 26 cycles a second, about the same frequency as a diesel engine. It is believed that the sound comes from the vibrations of the cat's larynx. A cat's meow is a unique sound and cats are able to make about 100 different vocalisations (compared with just 10 for dogs).

NOSE

- Cats can smell up to 14 times better than humans.

- They have somewhere from 60 million to 80 million olfactory cells; humans only have between 5 million and 20 million.

- Cats have about 24 movable whiskers, although some may have more. The whiskers are extremely sensitive, full of nerve endings that provide cats with information about the air around them and anything they touch. The whiskers, like the tail and ears, can also be an indicator of mood.

OTHER PHYSICAL FEATURES

- Cats use their tails for balance and the domestic cat is the only cat that is able to walk with its tail held straight up in the air.

- Cats sleep on average for 16 hours a day.

- Cats mark their territory using scent, either with the scent glands on their paws or by rubbing against things. So when a cat rubs itself against your knees, it is claiming ownership.

- Cats are very agile; they are able to turn the different halves of their bodies in different directions.

- It has been proven that stroking a cat can lower your blood pressure.

- Cats don't have a collarbone, which allows them to fit through any opening they can fit their head through.

- Cats can jump five times their height.

- Cats, like their owners, are righties or lefties; only 40% of cats are ambidextrous (compared with about 5% of humans).

Do cats always land on their feet?

This is a widely held belief, but this is not always the case! Cats have a reflex that allows them to twist their body using their heightened sense of agility and balance (mainly using their tail) in order to right themselves and land on their feet. Cats will always land on their feet, if they have time to do so (it is estimated that it takes seven stories for a cat to right itself).

Pocket fact ❖

The largest recorded cat weighed almost 47lbs, while the smallest weighed just 3lbs.

WHERE DOES THE WORD 'CAT' COME FROM?

This three-letter word has a big linguistic history.

The original roots of the word 'cat' stem, unsurprisingly, from the late Latin, *cattus*, meaning 'domestic cat' (not to be confused with *feles*, which denotes a wild cat). The list below illustrates the similarities between the term in many different languages:

Language	Word
Arabic	Kitte
Bulgarian	Kotka
Byzantine Greek	Kátia
Chinese	Miu or mau
Czech	Kocka
Danish	Kat
Dutch	Kat
Egyptian	Miw
English	Cat
Eskimo	Pussi
Estonian	Kass or kiisu
Farsi	Gorbe
Filipino	Cat or pusa
Finnish	Kissa
French	Chat
Gaelic	Pishyakan
German	Katze
Greek	Gatta
Hawaiian	Popoki
Hindi	Billi
Hungarian	Cica/macska
Icelandic	Kottur
Italian	Gatto

Language	Word
Japanese	Neko
Latin	Cattus
Malay/Indonesian	Kucing
Maltean	Gattus
Mayan	Miss
Netherlands	Kat (male); poes (female)
Norwegian	Katt
Norwegian	Katt
Old Irish	Cat
Polish	Kot
Portuguese	Gato
Romanian	Pisica
Russian	Koshka (female); kot (male)
Russian	Kot
Slovenian	Mačka; muca
Spanish	Gato
Swahili	Paka
Swedish	Katt
Thai/Vietnamese	Meo
Ukrainian	Kitska (female); kit (male)
Welsh	Cath
Yiddish	Kaz
Zulu	Ikati

The cat's miaow

Each cat's miaow is a unique sound and is described in a number of different languages:

- Mandarin Chinese: mao

- Japanese: nyaa, nyan

- Korean: yaong, nyaong

- Arabic: mowa'a

- Finnish: miau

- Egyptian: miw

- Italian: miao

- Greek: nicaou

Pocket fact ❖

CC (Copy Cat or Carbon Cat) was the first cloned cat in history. She was born using genetic technology at the College of Veterinary Medicine Texas A&M University in 2002. She is a brown tabby and white domestic shorthair and now lives in the household of one of the scientists who worked on the project. In September 2006, CC gave birth to three kittens who were fathered naturally.

🐾 CAT TERMINOLOGY 🐈

Pussycat hints at the femininity of felines, and comes from three possible sources:

- Low German: *puuskatte*
- Dialectical Swedish: *kattepus*
- Norwegian: *pusekatt*.

All of these refer to women and, by extension, cats.

Kitty is a term more widely used in American English, and comes, quite simply, from the word 'kitten'. It's also been adopted as a short version of the girl's name Katherine.

Moggies were once supposedly loose women or prostitutes, and it is thought that the name was used for female cats because of their tendency to mate repeatedly with different males and become pregnant by several different fathers simultaneously.

In Medieval English, kittens were often cutely called **catlings**.

There are many special words in use that denote specific felines, yet very few are actually in current use.

- A group of cats is actually called a **clowder**.
- A tomcat, once neutered, is a **gib**.
- Adult females are **queens**.
- When dealing with pedigrees, a male parent cat is a **sire**, and the female a **dam**.

An **ailurophile** is a person who loves cats. The word *ailuro* is from the ancient Greek word for cat.

Pocket fact 🐾

Antarctica is the only continent without a feline population.

✔ CATS AND THEIR NAMES ▶

Cats typically have very feline names – not many have human names, and most have a name related to their physical appearance, or a cute name. There is undeniably a collection of 'typical' cat names that just wouldn't fit any other species. A list of typical British moggy names includes:

- Poppy
- Mittens
- Tabby
- Sooty
- Blackie
- Ginger
- Cuddles
- Biscuit
- Smudge
- Marmalade

- Blossom
- Socks
- Garfield
- Sylvester
- Tigger
- Oscar
- Fluffy
- Dribbles
- Jasper
- Felix

Pocket tip 🧶

Looking for inspiration?

- *Search baby name listings*
- *Watch your favourite film*
- *Choose the name you always wanted for yourself*
- *Watch your kitten – does it show any strong characteristics or have distinct colourings?*
- *Take inspiration from flowers, food, history or other cultures*
- *Simply make a name up (see the bizarre cat name list below)!*

The most popular cat names in the UK

The RSPCA recently surveyed to find the 10 most common names for cats in the UK:

1. Molly
2. Felix
3. Smudge
4. Sooty
5. Tigger
6. Charlie
7. Alfie
8. Oscar
9. Millie
10. Misty

If you've tried to give your cat a less obvious name, you might be surprised that, for example, there are hundreds of feline Frodos and Bilbo Bagginses wandering around the streets of Britain already.

Pocket fact ❦

Bouhaki *is alleged to have been the first cat ever to be given a name. The name dates back to Egyptian writings of 2000BC. In hieroglyphics,* bou *means 'house' and* hak *was the symbol for 'divine ruler'.*

Here's a list of some of the more bizarre names that owners have given their cats, to get your imagination flowing.

- Admiral Snuggles
- Alf Schnitzelburg
- Archie the Magical Rhino
- Aspirin
- Bananas
- Bob
- Bojangles
- BT (British Telecom)
- Carwash
- Couch potato
- Dennis the Menace
- DOG
- Frag Schnaggler
- George of the Jungle
- Ham
- Hot Dog the Mystical Raccoon
- Jellybean Pizza
- Jimmy the Robot
- Mr. Nincompoop
- Mr. Tiddybomboms
- Optimus Prime

- Pawlette
- Pedro Megatron
- Prince Humperdinck
- Salami
- Schrodinger
- Sir Odd-Face
- Sir Winklebottom the Grand
- Sparta
- The Ugliest Cat I've Ever Seen
- Tummysticks
- Winky Woozerton
- Zaphod Beeblebrox

Pocket tip 🐾

If you're looking for a funny name for your cat, use the prefixes: Mr, Mrs, Miss, Doctor, Sir, Lady, Admiral, Lord or Captain, and it's sure to raise a smile!

Famous owners and their alternative cat names

- *Frank Bruno — Del Boy*
- *Winston Churchill — Jock, Mr Cat*
- *Charles Dickens — The Master's Cat*
- *TS Eliot — Jellylorum*
- *Thomas Hardy — Kiddleywinkempoops*
- *Ernest Hemingway — Fats, Crazy Christian, Furhouse, Friendless Brother, Thruster, Willy and Mr Feather Puss*
- *Florence Nightingale — Jock and Margate (but she did name the other two Bob and Blackie . . .)*
- *Poet Robert Southby — Rumpel, full name: The Most Noble the Archduke Rumpelstizchen, Marquis Macbum, Earle Tomemange, Baron Raticide, Waowler, and Skaratchi*
- *Mark Twain — Zoroaster, Apollinaris, Beelzebub, Blatherskite, Buffalo Bill, Sour Mash, Tammany, and Sin*
- *US President Jimmy Carter — Misty Malarky and Ying Yang*
- *Martha Stewart — Beethoven, Mozart, Verdi and Vivaldi*
- *Jay Leno — Cheeses*
- *HG Wells — Mr Peter Wells*
- *Doris Day — Punky*

🐈 WHY OWN A CAT? 🐈

'Dogs have owners. Cats have staff.'
Anonymous

Cats are officially the UK's most popular pet, having stolen the title from dogs in about 2002 due to changing lifestyles of the British public. Cats replaced dogs in the popularity charts, as they're easier to care for, intelligent and require relatively little of their owner's time.

Giving a home to a cat can be every bit as beneficial to you as it is to your cat. Owning a moggy isn't all about responsibility, planning holidays and catteries well in advance, and worrying about her diet and safety: the benefits of owning a cat are considerable.

People choose to share their homes with cats for a variety of reasons, the most popular being the following:

- Love (31%)

- Companionship (27%)

- Easy maintenance (7%)

- Cats get along well with other species (3%).

Pocket fact 🐾
2.5 million 18–29-year-olds in the UK own a pet for companionship, and look forward to coming home to their cat or dog after long working hours.

The battle of the sexes

- *Cats respond better to women than to men, as due to the higher pitch of women's voices, they probably appear to be friendlier and less frightening.*
- *Some cats are so frightened of men that they run and hide at the sound of a male stranger's voice, and can stay hidden away for days.*
- *It has been suggested that men who keep cats are up to 80% more attractive to women.*

Pocket fact ❧

A tabby cat called Towser was put in charge of rodent control in the Glenturret Distillery in Scotland and over her 21 year career killed over 28,899 mice.

Numerous studies have been conducted to find out how owning a cat affects owners. Here are some of the findings:

- Caring for a pet together strengthens the bond between a couple, as it provides a common focus and object for love and affection away from busy working lives.

- Unburdening oneself to a cat can be even more therapeutic than talking to a friend or partner about worries.

- Having a cat has a real effect on quality of life. Elderly cat owners have more physical activity, and research has proved that this helps with the release of 'happy chemicals' such as serotonin and the endorphins released after exercise.

- Children with pets have a greater sense of responsibility, better social skills, higher attendance rates at school, and a happier, more relaxed attitude towards life in general.

- Some studies have even shown that introducing children to cats at a young age can help build up resistance against asthma and allergens.

Pocket fact ❖

Ninety-eight per cent of British cat-owning children claim to play with their cat every day.

- Sharing your home with a cat can actually reduce the winter blues and SAD (seasonal affective disorder). A study carried out by the Cats Protection League claimed that cat owners are about 20% less likely to catch colds and flu, and even have fewer headaches than those without cats, by up to 60%.

- Cats can be therapeutic and calming. Their response to affection from anybody is reassuring, and this is why they make excellent nursing home pets. Stroking a cat can provide much-needed relief for the old and infirm, and there have even been cases reported which tell of the company of cats evoking long-lost memories in Alzheimer sufferers, bringing happiness to hospices and homes.

Pocket fact ❖

Cat owners are 24% less stressed than dog owners, according to a recent survey by the Cats Protection League.

The cat with no face

In the USA, the 'cat with no face' helps those who have become disfigured in accidents. The black and white moggy, Chase, was run over by a car at a young age, and survived the ordeal but now has nothing but pink flesh and two eyes where his furry face should be. Despite initial belief that nobody would care for him and he would have to be put down, the vet who helped him survive adopted him, and he is now not only happy and healthy, but has an online blog and also goes visiting humans with disabilities and disfigurements, in a bid to reassure them that it is okay to be different.

A SHORT HISTORY OF CATS

EGYPTIANS AND THEIR FELINE SAVIOURS

*'Many years ago, cats were worshipped as gods. Cats have
never forgotten this.'*
Terry Pratchett

The relationship between cats and humans stretches back as far as
3000BC, when Egyptians recognised that the furry little creatures
sharing their world were not without their uses.

History has it that Ancient Egyptian cities were swarming
with hungry mice and rats, whose desperate nibbling at the
food stored in woven baskets left the residents with very little
to eat.

By coincidence, the equally hungry African wildcat came and
feasted upon the rodents. This ancestor of the modern-day pussycat was quickly recognised by the Egyptians as a saviour, restoring
order to the chaos that had governed their lives, and placing food
back on the table.

As an act of gratitude, residents of the city left titbits for their new
feline friends, and the cats consequently kept returning, growing
fatter and more well-fed by the day.

Respect and love for felines grew to the extent that they were soon
accorded a status almost equal to that of their owners, often being
mummified and buried alongside them.

Pocket fact ❀

The Egyptians held cats in such high esteem that they buried them with mummified rats, mice, and even saucers of food. By the time the African wildcat had evolved into the Egyptian Mau, it was considered as an embodiment of Egyptian gods, and the penalty for killing a cat was instant death.

CATS GO GLOBAL

The Egyptians' love of cats quickly spread to other parts of the world, despite Egyptian law stating that cats were not permitted to leave the country. Unsurprisingly, the price fetched for such creatures was high, and inhabitants of both Europe and Asia happily invested in acquiring felines of their own.

Sales increased to the Romans, Celts, Gaels and other Europeans, and the worldwide pet cat emerged.

DARK TIMES IN THE MIDDLE AGES

Cats had a tough time of it in the Middle Ages, as Europeans believed their species was closely associated with the devil: they faced horrifying punishments for their associations with black magic, from being burned at the stake and tried before judges (even without their owners!) to being buried alive inside walls of new buildings.

Pocket fact ❀

In ancient Egypt, entire families would shave their eyebrows as a sign of mourning when the family cat died!

Pocket fact ❧

The first record of cats being present in the UK goes back to AD936, when the Welsh king Hywel Dda (literally 'Good Howell') passed legislation making it illegal to kill or harm a cat.

Cats eventually shed their association with evil and witchcraft. It was also recognised that treating these innocent and useful rat-catchers with such unfounded cruelty had led to the spread of the plague, and as this became more obvious, remorseful humans once again treated them with respect. The cat began to enjoy the status to which it is now accustomed: that of cherished yet independent pet.

By the 17th century, it was considered fashionable to own a cat. A notable example is that of Cardinal Richelieu, a distinguished Frenchman who owned numerous cats in his lifetime and even built a cattery in Versailles to house them all.

Pocket fact ❧

According to 17th-century folklore, cats suffocate newborn babies by putting their noses to the child's mouth, sucking its breath out. This is, of course, entirely untrue!

OVERPOPULATION

Sadly, the sheer number of cats causes huge problems, as feral and wild cats will continue to reproduce to the point of serious overpopulation unless control is taken and they get spayed. Every new litter makes a real difference and adds to this problem: one single unspayed female producing four kittens a year and just two female kittens per litter can cause the birth of over 10,000 cats in seven years!

Pocket fact ❧

There are now more than nine million cats in the UK, meaning that roughly one in every seven people owns a cat. The south-east is home to half of the UK's cat population. More than 1 billion cats exist worldwide.

The hero of the seas

The old story of the Able Seacat Simon tells of how an entire ship of sailors was saved by one moggy. Legend has it that in 1948, HMS Amethyst set sail with a cat smuggled on board. When Simon was discovered, there was outrage — until the sailors realised he was catching and killing all of the rats on board. Rats gnawed away at food supplies and deprived sailors of the nutrition they desperately needed, so Simon became invaluable. In 1949, though, the ship came under fire from the Communists, and most of the crew, including Simon, were injured. Because most of the men were taken off board to hospitals, the ship's doctor was able to attend to Simon when he emerged from his hiding place two days later, and he was quickly healed. By carrying on catching rats, he saved the remaining crew from starvation, and was awarded the PDSA Dickin Medal for service of the highest order. His grave is in Ilford, and the headstone outlines his brave feline achievements.

🐈 BREEDS OF CAT 🐈

There are two kinds of cat: the domestic, common cat, and pedigree breeds. The IPCBA (International Progressive Cat Breeders Alliance) currently recognises 73 breeds, while the CFA (Cat Fanciers' Association) only recognises 41.

THE COMMON CAT

Common cats are those that do not have a traceable lineage, ie they are not pedigreed. There are several terms that can refer to the common cat:

- the domestic cat (which can be further broken down into domestic shorthair, domestic longhair and domestic mediumhair)

- house cat

- moggy

- alley cat

- mixed breed.

As common cats have no discernable breed lineage, it is easier to categorise them in terms of colour.

The colour of a cat is determined by its genetic makeup. A mother cat can give birth to a whole range of kittens (tabby, calico, etc), depending on her own genetic make-up and that of the father.

Cats come in three basic colours: ginger, black and white. The most common colour patterns for cats are:

- tabby

- solids

- tri-colour cats, including calico and tortoiseshell

- tuxedo

- bi-colour

- points.

> *Pocket fact* ❀
>
> *The first glow-in-the-dark cat, Mr Green Genes, is the result of a genetic experiment at an American university. He appears to be an ordinary moggy until placed under ultraviolet light, when his eyes, gums and tongue glow a vivid lime green. This has not become a recognised breed!*

It is important to remember that these types of common cat are not breeds of cat, merely a distinction by coat pattern. For example, the gene for the tabby pattern can be found in all cat breeds.

Tabby

Tabby cats are commonly recognised by the stripes, dots or swirls on their coats. There are four distinctive patterns found in tabbies (although there can be several combinations and varieties of these):

- mackerel (vertical, curving stripes)

- classic (swirl pattern with wider stripes)

- ticked (different colours in each individual hair, giving a shimmering or salt-and-pepper appearance)

- spotted (like it says on the tin, spotted).

Apart from their pattern, the most distinctive feature of a tabby cat is the 'M' on their forehead. Some claim that this M came from the prophet Mohammed as he rested his hand on his favourite cat. Others tell the story that at the birth of Jesus, a tabby curled up next to the baby to keep him warm and the Virgin Mary bestowed her initial on the cat.

The tabby coat has its origins in wild cats, and is seen on big cats such as tigers. And indeed the term 'tabby' has for many people an association with tough, alley cats. The owners of tabbies will assure you of their loving nature, though.

Pocket fact ❖

A cat's nose pat has a unique pattern, just like a human fingerprint.

Tortoiseshell and calico

These are two very similar colour patterns and are often confused. The main difference between the two patterns is that tortoiseshell cats have orange and brown mixed together in their coat, and usually less white. Calico cats have a white background with separate sections of black, brown and orange.

To be a calico, a cat must have a tri-coloured coat pattern. It is the mixture of colours that distinguishes the tortoiseshell cat. Some cats can have a mixture of both patterns, explaining the confusion.

This type of cat is nearly always female. Male tortoiseshell or calico cats are very rare (about 1 in 3,000) and they are most often sterile. This is due to the genetic make-up of this colour pattern. These cats are often thought to be good luck, and in Japan calico cats were believed to protect sailors at sea. The calico was adopted by Maryland as its state cat in 2001.

Pocket fact ❧

White cats, if they have blue eyes, are up to 85% more likely to be deaf due to a hereditary condition.

Why own a moggy?

Around 90% of the cats in the UK are moggies, and aside from the cost of some pedigree breeds, moggies can be wonderful pets with interesting personalities and colour patterns. The main issue when choosing to own a common cat is that you don't know where it has come from, meaning you have no indication of its background or any clue as to how big it will grow, any genetic health problems, etc.

Pocket tip ❧

When choosing a mixed breed cat as a pet, it is sometimes a good idea to choose an adult cat from a shelter because then you can be sure of its size and personality.

Some people claim that mixed breed cats can be more robust, suffer fewer inherited problems and may even live longer than their pedigree counterparts. Ninety-seven per cent of cat owners in the UK own a common moggy.

PEDIGREE CATS

A pedigree cat is a feline with a known line of descent, whose parents and grandparents can be traced back for at least four generations. They are carefully bred to ensure a pure bloodline, and in the UK can fetch a price of anything from £300 upwards.

Pocket fact ❧

Breeding and registering pedigree cats is a hobby known as the 'Cat Fancy'. Most pedigree cats in the UK are registered with the GCCF — the Governing Council of the Cat Fancy.

Owning pedigree cats

Why own a pedigree cat as opposed to a fluffy mongrel?
Initial reasons are quite superficial: some pedigrees are very pretty (the Persian, for example). Many owners make a living from breeding pedigree cats, whilst others derive great pleasure from attending cat shows and spending time with other like-minded ailurophiles.

Special considerations
Contrary to what most people think, pedigrees aren't actually much more difficult to care for than ordinary cats.

- Long-haired breeds do require careful brushing and combing every day, but they otherwise require warm beds, good meals and affection.

- Some breeds do need a slightly warmer environment, especially those with very short hair, which are built very differently from the average solid British housecat. Siamese and Orientals, for example, like to sleep under duvets, against radiators, in airing cupboards . . . many owners invest in electrically heated pads for such breeds.

Pocket fact ❧

Pedigree cats are 34% more expensive to own than common breeds.

- Many feline advisory boards suggest keeping pedigrees indoors all day and only allowing them outside whilst the owner is at home, to ensure that they will not run away.

- Most owners of pedigree cats also tend to constrict the outside areas the cat can go to, to protect them from other animals and danger.

Only 3% of the nation's cat owners actually own a pedigree cat.

Pocket fact ❀

The most expensive cat ever to have been bought costs £12,000. Bred by British businessman Simon Brodie, it is more than 1 metre tall on its hind legs, and weighs over 30lbs. Named the Ashera, it sells because of its beautiful tiger markings and calm temperament.

The problems of pedigree

Pedigrees, in any species, are subject to the dangers of inbreeding. Weaknesses that are present in a particular breed will become increasingly noticeable (and increasingly serious) as more generations are born.

- *Cats that suffer the most from inbreeding in the UK include Persians (one of the most popular breeds) and the Sphynx, both of which are subject to uncomfortable health problems associated with their particular breed.*
- *Persians are bred to have a flat face, which may look cute but actually causes the breed a lot of problems. Their eyes*

tend to bulge out of their head and weep constantly, meaning that owners are constantly wiping them.
- Sphynx cats suffer from the cold in winter and sunburn in summer because of their short coat.
- Burmese cats suffer from pain in their faces leading to scratching, and Siamese cats are particularly prone to lung cancer.
- Munchkin cats have very short legs and suffer from joint problems as a result, and Scottish Fold cats have a characteristic bent ear caused by a genetic defect, which causes them to suffer cartilage problems around their bodies.

Pocket fact ❧

The richest cat in the world is Blackie who inherited £15 million, left to him by British recluse Ben Rea.

Breeds of pedigree cat

Abyssinian

The earliest mention of an Abyssinian in the UK on record was in 1872. Abyssinians are 'people cats' and love company, although they are not lap-cats. They have thin necks and pointy ears, and comparatively large bodies. They aren't used as show cats very often, because despite being generally friendly and in need of attention, they are timid around strangers. Abyssinians get on well with other cats, but the females can become irritable and need their space sometimes.

Birman

The Birman is a very pretty breed of cat with soft golden fluffy fur and big blue eyes. They are born white, but their coat develops and becomes either seal-point (gold with dark brown markings) or blue-point (eggshell coat and blue markings). They originate from Burma, but should not be confused with the Burmese breed. Birmans are friendly and affectionate, but never attention-seeking.

Pocket fact ❧

Mark Twain, author of Huckleberry Finn, thought that cats were better than people. He famously said: 'Of all God's creatures, there is only one that cannot be made the slave of the leash. That one is the cat. If man could be crossed with the cat it would improve man, but it would deteriorate the cat.'

British Shorthair

The British Shorthair is easy-going, intelligent, and very popular in the UK. It is solidly built and quite easy to care for, and although not very athletic, the British Shorthair is a favourite for film and television use due to good behaviour. Males weigh up to 10kg, and females up to 7kg.

Burmese

Burmese cats gravitate towards human activity, forming strong bonds with their owners. They are near-perfect pets, tolerant of children and dogs (and in fact, almost dog-like themselves in their loving habits). Their most distinctive feature is their huge eyes, but they should never be allowed outside as they have no survival instinct, believing that the way to overcome difficulties is simply to make eyes at predators.

Cornish Rex

Cornish Rex cats are often referred to as the 'greyhounds of the cat world'. They are relatively small and skinny, and only have a thin undercoat of hair – this means that they gravitate towards warm areas and crave heat. They often emit a faintly cheesy odour unique to the breed, which comes from scent glands in their paws. Intelligent and adventurous, it is friendly and gets along well with most species.

Egyptian Mau
The Egyptian Mau is an ancestor of the modern domestic cat, and was once deified and worshipped in Egypt, being mummified when it died. It is the only naturally spotted breed of domestic feline, and displays lots of affection and loyalty to those around it. The Mau (the Egyptian word for cat) is also highly intelligent, and their musical voices make chirruping noises unique to their breed.

Pocket fact ❀

The largest cat breed is the Ragdoll, while the Singapura is the smallest.

Japanese Bobtail
Japanese Bobtails, as the name suggests, have tails that resemble those of rabbits more than the typical cat. Their tails are no longer than 3in in length due to a recessive gene. They were once the street cats of Japan, as law stated that none could be sold or kept as pets because their job was rat-catching. Most can be trained to play fetch, and they enjoy carrying things in their mouths. Bobtails are very friendly and love human company.

Maine Coon
Maine Coons are very popular in the USA, and are becoming increasingly so in Britain. They are big, heavy, sturdy cats with

huge fluffy tails and a ruffle of fur around their neck. They originate from Maine in the USA, and are the second most popular
breed in the world. Maine Coons are probably the result of the
breeding of domestic cats from the area and long-haired felines
brought by travellers. This hasn't dispelled the myth that the cats
are bred from domestic shorthairs and raccoons, though – an
attractive and interesting idea that is actually genetically impossible, but remains popular because of their huge tails (and huge
build in general). They are very friendly cats, and get along with
other animals, humans and especially children.

Pocket fact ❖

*Kittens with six toes have become so common in Boston and
Massachusetts that they are now an established mutation.*

Manx
The Manx cat is tail-less, and originates from the Isle of Man. It
doesn't have problems with balance, though, and is generally quite
a healthy breed. The hind legs of a Manx are longer than the front
legs, meaning that it has a slight hop: this combined with the lack
of tail has elicited suggestions that a Manx is a cross between a
cat and rabbit. This is biologically impossible, though, and it is
difficult to tell where the breed actually originated due to the
vast number of ships that docked on the Isle in the past and
could have brought the parent cat from overseas. They are a
sturdy breed, and dog-like in many ways: from their loyalty to
their tendency to bury their toys.

Pocket fact ❖

Some cruel breeders dock ordinary kittens' tails and attempt to sell them as Manx cats.

Persian

The Persian is one of the most popular breeds of pedigree cat. Docile and good-natured, the Persian adapts to almost any home environment, and although not particularly playful makes a lovely pet. It does require a lot of care, though: regular bathing is essential, as is daily combing of its long coat. Contrary to popular belief, not all Persians are white – they exist in many different colours; it's just that the white is more frequently photographed.

Siamese

Despite its skinny, somewhat awkward appearance, the Siamese is the most popular breed of pedigree cat in the UK. It arrived in the 1800s and was a gift from an emperor of Thailand (then Siam). The best-known variety is the seal point, and this exists in various colours; the traditional darkest brown, blue, chocolate and lilac. Their elongated features give them a real air of elegance, added to by their silky short coats and deep blue eyes. Siamese cats aren't at all snobby, though, and often attach themselves to one particular person (whilst remaining friendly with all others). Their short coats make them easy to care for.

Are Siamese cats cruel?

The Siamese may be one of the more well-known breeds of cat, but it has received some bad press over the years. The most notorious example featured in the Disney film *Lady and the Tramp*, and for many generations of children since the 1980s, the piano scene will cement the breed in their young minds as devious, sly and spiteful. The famous, 'We are Siamese if you please' song is one that everybody remembers, but the breed is actually very friendly.

Sphynx

The Sphynx cat is hairless – its most famous attribute. The skin is not smooth like human skin, though; it is warm and feels almost like a peach. Sphynx cats tend to show off for attention and follow their owners around in pursuit of it, probably equally because they are in constant pursuit of warmth, especially in winter. Like the Cornish Rex, they suffer from sunburn, and need appropriate care to ensure that they are always warm – but never too warm! The Sphynx is thought to be Canadian, and requires frequent bathing because the oils that build up naturally on the skin of cats are not absorbed by a furry coat.

Pocket fact ❧

Only 3% of pet cats in the UK are pedigree breeds, yet there are around 40 breeds of pedigree cat recognised by the Feline Advisory Bureau.

The most popular pedigree cats in the UK are:

- Siamese
- Bengal

- British Shorthair
- Burmese
- Manx.

Cat shows

In the UK, the Governing Council of the Cat Fancy determines cat breeds and decides which are eligible for showing.

The first ever cat show was held in 1871 at Crystal Palace.

The biggest cat show in the UK is the Supreme Cat Show, held in Birmingham at the NEC. It's a fancy, glossy affair, and everyone who's anyone in the cat fancying world should be there. More than 1,000 cats are shown at this event annually, of all shapes and sizes. There are numerous other cat shows across the country, too, from those held in big cities to little village pet shows.

Cat shows tend to be held by cat clubs and associations in each area or region of the UK, and aren't just for pedigree cats; they exist for moggies too. These shows tend to be a less glamorous affair, though, and less strict attention is paid to the criteria used to judge the animals.

Cats are judged on prescribed physical criteria, and although these vary from breed to breed, there are some basic requirements. These include the following:

- coat
- eyes
- teeth
- claws
- general health

ABOUT CATS • 35

- *proportions*
- *personality*
- *fitness.*

As a general rule, judges look for breed standard. Originality and quirkiness just aren't rewarded in this environment – it's all about conforming to a perfect standard.

- *Awards come in the form of rosettes, and these are placed on the cage at the show.*
- *Even if you don't have a pedigree cat to show and you're happily in love with your own scruffy little moggy, attending a show can be a really interesting experience. The sight of hundreds of perfectly groomed, highly bred cats sitting pretty really is incredible, whether you agree with breeding or not.*

Pocket fact ❖

Since 1979, Florence Groff of France has amassed a record-breaking collection of 11,717 cat-related items. Among the collection are 2,118 different cat figurines (48 of which are fridge magnets), 86 decorative plates, 60 pieces of crystalware, 140 metallic boxes, 9 lamps, 36 stuffed toys, 41 painted eggs, and 2,666 pussy postcards.

Wild cats

Even in the UK one might encounter a wild cat. Deep in the Scottish highlands, undisturbed by civilisation, they still roam the hills. Being extremely timid, very few are ever seen by human eyes, yet each tends to inhabit a territory of approximately 3 sq km, living solitarily and avoiding contact with all living beings except for its prey.

Despite their relatively similar appearance, the differences between the wild cat and domestic cat are huge.

- In sharp contrast to the nine million domestic cats in the UK, the Scottish wild cat is the most endangered carnivore in the country; there are only around 500 left altogether.
- The lives they lead are also very different. Far from the comforts of cat food and comfy sofas, wild cats stalk and kill prey, sleeping it off afterwards in the cold rough terrain of the Scottish highlands.
- Living in such conditions clearly makes the wild cat very robust; it has to survive freezing cold snowy winters, making do with what nature provides as a shelter.
- There are around 40 species of wild and big cat that don't fall into the categories of moggy or pedigree, including lions and tigers.
- Wild cats that don't extend into the big cat family can be found in Scotland, Africa, Asia and other parts of Europe. Wild cats are under threat in all of these countries.
- They can weigh anything from 6lbs to 18lbs, and tend to measure between 18in and 32in.

❧ LIFESPAN OF CATS ❧

- The average lifespan is 14 years.

- A cat can live to as much as 25 years, but this is dependent on genetic factors as well as other factors such as diet and lifestyle.

- The first two years of a cat's life are crucial as a little kitten ages very quickly: by the age of two it is considered a fully fledged adult.

- The first year of a cat's life is about the equivalent to 15 human years, and their second year is about the same as nine human years.

- After these first two years, a cat ages four human years for every one cat year (roughly). So a cat that makes it to the age of 20 is the equivalent of a 96-year-old human.

Pocket fact ❀

Domestic moggies tend to live longer than pedigrees.

How old is your cat in human terms?

To figure out your cat's age: count their first year as 15, count their second year as 9, and multiply their remaining number of years by 4. Here's an example:

A cat who has lived for 13 years is in fact 68:

$$(15+9+(11\times4) = 68).$$

There are several factors that can have an impact on a cat's life expectancy.

- There are differences in the life expectancy of an indoor cat (one who is never allowed to go outside) as opposed to a cat who does venture outdoors.

- The average life span of an outdoor cat can be as little as six years, but some people feel the exercise and freedom they enjoy is crucial to their well-being. The brevity of an outdoor cat's life expectancy is mainly due to the risks presented to outdoor cats, such as exposure to disease or road accidents.

- There also seems to be a shorter life expectancy rate for pedigree cats as their selective breeding makes them prone to certain illnesses or afflictions, unlike their more hardy moggy counterparts.

- It has also been found that neutered or spayed cats live longer than those who have not undergone one of these procedures.

Essentially, though, if you look after your cat and provide the right kind of diet and exercise, they should live a long healthy life.

Pocket fact ❖

The oldest cat ever was Crème Puff from Austin, Texas. He was born in 1967 and died in 2005, making him 38 years old.

The oldest pedigree cat ever to have lived was a Sphynx called Granpa. He lived to the age of 34.

HOW CAN YOU TELL THE AGE OF A CAT?

Teeth: This is done by examining both the degree of growth in the teeth, and how worn they are. Some factors may affect the result: cats who have received good dental care will appear to be younger, and teeth really do just provide a rough indication of age when there is no other alternative.

Fur: Fur will probably become thinner (and occasionally duller). Combing to reduce matting is essential, and owners need to be vigilant and seek veterinary advice at the first signs of any lumps or bumps on the skin. Black cats may develop flecks of grey or white in their coat.

The Cat with Nine Lives

Cats are always getting themselves in and out of scrapes, climbing trees or walking along rooftops – they are intrepid explorers and fearless acrobats. Every time they get themselves out of danger, they are said to have lost one of their nine lives. According to Brewer's Dictionary Of Phrase & Fable, *a cat is said to have nine lives because it is 'more tenacious of life than many animals'. But why the number nine?*

Nine, a trinity of trinities, is a mystical number often invoked in religion and folklore. The cat was once revered in Egypt, and this is probably where its nine lives began. Atum-Ra, an Egyptian sun god who took the form of a cat for visits to the underworld, embodied nine lives in one creator, and this is probably where the saying came from.

Nails: Nails can become brittle, and may need careful trimming as older, less mobile cats will be less inclined to use scratching posts.

Mobility: Perhaps the most obvious sign of ageing is decreased mobility: this may sound obvious, but, like humans, cats become arthritic and tired with old age.

HOW DOES AGEING AFFECT CATS?

Muscles fade and grow less strong as they are used progressively less, and care must be taken to ensure that litter trays and all food bowls are accessible – accidents and hungry wailing cats are not an attractive prospect!

Kidneys and the liver may become old and less able to carry out their jobs within the body, and both hearing and eyesight may also deteriorate. All of this indicates an ageing cat, and he or she should receive extra love, care and attention in their later years to ensure that they are happy ones!

WHAT HELPS CATS TO LIVE LONGER?

Conditions that all cats need to stay healthy and live longer include the following:

- healthy diet
- exercise
- good health care
- safe environment
- good genes.
- Indoor domestic cats tend to survive longer than wild ones simply because they are much more sheltered from predators and other dangers of the outside world.

- Pedigrees tend to be subject to illnesses that result from inbreeding (see p. 28), and for this reason they live slightly shorter lives than their mongrel counterparts on the whole.

- Cats are natural predators and carnivores, and should be encouraged from an early age to chase prey, run outside and exercise.

- A varied diet is essential in increasing lifespan – these little predators aren't supposed to survive on crunchy cat biscuits.

- Overfeeding your cat can result in a short lifespan. Turn to p. 125 for more on how you can ensure that your cat's healthy.

Pocket fact ❖

An old wives' tale states that black cats live longer than white cats. This is still believed by some older generations, but evidence suggests that it is in no way true. The myth probably originated because white cats are less easily camouflaged from predators and are therefore hunted and killed that little bit more easily.

2

CATS IN CULTURE

🐈 LITERATURE 🐈

Since storytelling began, cats have always played a role, and tend to emerge as history portrayed them at the time: godlike in Egyptian times, evil in the Middle Ages, faithful companions afterwards. We've included some of the most famous cats immortalised in literature.

DICK WHITTINGTON'S CAT

The famous cat belonging to Dick Whittington was supposedly sent away to sea by its owner when he had no choice. He had saved up all of the pennies he earned shining shoes to buy his feline friend. Once he had bought the cat, Dick slept soundly in his pauper's room, because he was no longer plagued by the rats running all over him in his sleep, yet one day his landlord sent a ship to sea and asked that all those who worked for him place an object that could be exchanged for money on board. Dick had nothing but his cat, and his heart broke as he placed his only friend aboard a ship destined for faraway lands, never to be seen again.

TOM KITTEN

Beatrix Potter's Tom Kitten is a delightfully naughty little tomcat, who leads his sisters Mittens and Moppet astray. Their mother,

Mrs Tabitha Twitchit, is hosting a fancy tea party, and dresses the three kittens up accordingly. Tom Kitten has become very fat, though, and all the buttons pop off his blue suit. His mother sews them back on, and sends the three outside out of the way. Tom Kitten naughtily gives his suit to Mr Drake Puddle-Duck, and his sisters shed their little outfits too. When they return home, Mrs Twitchit is furious and sends the three upstairs, telling her fancy guests that the kittens have measles.

Edward Lear's Pussycat

The Pussycat from *The Owl and the Pussycat*, 1871, is one of the most famous in children's literature. The poem tells of a cat and an owl falling in love and sailing away in a 'beautiful pea-green boat'. Loaded with honey and money, they sail away and are married by a turkey in the 'land where the bong-tree grows'. A pig sells them his nose-ring to use as a wedding ring, and they happily buy it, desperate to be man and wife (or, indeed, owl and cat). The poem ends with the pair dining upon mince and dancing together in the moonlight, and despite the sheer absurdity of the tale it remains one of the most popular in English literature.

Pocket fact ❧

A cat called Hamlet escaped from his carrier while on a flight from Toronto. When he was found 7 weeks later hiding behind a panel he had travelled almost 375,000 miles!

The Cheshire Cat

Lewis Carroll created the grinning Cheshire Cat in *Alice in Wonderland*, 1865. Based on the British shorthair breed, he is a sturdy, cobby cat; well built with a huge smile. He first meets Alice in the Duchess' kitchen, then again outside, up a tree. The cat vexes Alice with its disappearing acts, yet amuses her at the same time.

Amid philosophical debates, the cat performs tricks and makes Alice laugh. At one point he makes all of his body disappear except for his huge grin. When sentenced to death, he cleverly makes his body disappear, leaving the King and Queen arguing over whether it is possible to behead an animal without a body . . .

PUSS IN BOOTS

Puss in Boots has enjoyed a boost in popularity amongst younger generations today due to his hilarious performance in the recent *Shrek* films. Traditionally, Puss in Boots is a clever, scheming cat who works to help his master achieve fame and fortune. In the popular fairytale, a miller's son is left with nothing but the supposedly worthless granary cat upon his father's death. Bitterly disappointed, he contemplates eating the cat to at least get some use out of it. The cat begs and pleads with him not to, claiming that in return for a pair of boots and a cloth sack, he will make his master rich. The boy accepts, reluctantly.

The cat's first triumph is filling the sack with pheasants, partridges and other game and presenting it to the King. He then engineers a situation that results in the miller's son being dressed up in regal clothes and taken to the palace, because he is naked in the river with supposedly stolen clothes at the exact moment the King passes by (the cat actually steals the clothes, knowing what will happen). This leads eventually to the miller's boy owning land and marrying a princess.

Pocket fact ❖

Some house plants can be poisonous to cats such as the Philodendron. The leaves of the Easter Lily can cause permanent and life-threatening kidney damage to cats.

THE CAT THAT WALKED BY HIMSELF

Rudyard Kipling's famous solitary cat appears in a poem of the same name written in 1902. The story tells of how humans and animals came together and made friends, but implies that the cat had a difficult time doing so.

According to the story, when man met woman they went to live in a cave, and gradually accepted dogs, horses and cows into the fold. They seemed to hate the cat, though, and the woman told it that unless she praised it three times it would not be allowed in to drink the cow's milk. The cat carried on walking by himself, but was relentless and continued trying to get into the cave. The woman had a baby, and the cat knew that this was a big opportunity for him. He made friends with it, stopped it crying, and killed a mouse – enough action to elicit sufficient praise from the woman to enter the cave.

Pocket fact ❧

Perhaps the most famous 'bad cat' is the Grimalkin. Felines of this name appear throughout history and literature, from Nostradamus' cat and the cat that accompanies the three witches at the beginning of Shakespeare's Macbeth to those featured in Henry Fielding's Tom Jones and Emily Brontë's Wuthering Heights. Not one is portrayed in a positive light, and almost all are grey, mangy and evil she-cats!

Villainous cats
There seems to be an equal number of films which depict cats as the villains, though.

- The Bond villain Blofeld in the movie *You Only Live Twice* is shown as stroking a white Persian cat, an image of a super villain that has become a common cliché, for example as demonstrated by Mike Myers' character Dr Evil in the *Austin Powers* films.

- In the children's film *Cats and Dogs*, cats are portrayed as the ultimate super villains.

- In many other children's films cats are the 'bad guys', such as Lucifer in *Cinderella* and the Siamese cats in *Lady and the Tramp*.

There are also several characters who have appeared over the years that invoke feline feelings. The most famous of these is perhaps the character of Catwoman in the Batman films. The role was originally played by Michelle Pfeifer and then reprised in a spin-off film with Halle Berry in the starring role.

OTHER CATS FOUND IN WORKS OF LITERATURE

- **The Cat in the Hat** is a children's book by Dr. Seuss, featuring a tall, anthropomorphic, mischievous cat, wearing a tall, red and white striped hat, and a bowtie. He also carries an umbrella.

- **Dinah:** Alice's cat. Dinah is very good at hunting and killing animals, a fact that Alice can't seem to keep to herself. This is most embarrassing when she is in the company of a great many animals who are horrified (rather than impressed) by the notion of a Cat Hunter.

- Laura's cat, **Kitty**, is from *The Little House on the Prairie* books. She appeared in the TV series of the same name in an episode entitled 'Days of Sunshine, Days of Shadow'.

- The **MEG & MOG** stories have become classics, thanks to exuberant illustrations and crazy story lines. They follow the antics of Meg, the witch whose spells usually end in disaster, and Mog, her long-suffering cat.

- **Crookshanks:** Hermione Granger's cat in the *Harry Potter* books may be the bane of Ron's (and Scabbers') life, but he is always helpful in spotting the untrustworthy characters.

- Again in the *Harry Potter* books, **Mrs Norris** is a smart (but unpleasant) cat under the care of Argus Filch. She has bulging yellow, lamp-like eyes, a scrawny, skeletal body and dust-coloured fur. Like her owner, she roams the Hogwarts Castle hallways in search of troublemakers.

- *Old Possum's Book of Practical Cats* is a collection of whimsical poems by T. S. Eliot about feline psychology and sociology. Its contents are widely known as the basis for the record-setting musical *Cats*.

Pocket fact ❧

Author Raymond Chandler used to call Taki, his black female Persian cat, his 'secretary', and he always read her the first drafts of his crime novels.

🐈 MYTH 🐈

Cats appear in myth just as much as they do in literature. The black cat is especially famous, as a symbol of both good and bad luck, and felines tend to be figures of mystery and magic.

Below are some myths and superstitions surrounding cats, black or otherwise:

- Black cats are only considered lucky in the UK and Asia. Elsewhere, they either don't represent anything or are unlucky.

- A festival was recently held in Italy to promote the black cat and rescue it from the bad press and, consequently, even the abuse that it suffers.

Pocket fact 🐾

Some Italians still believe that the presence of a black cat on the bed of a sick person will result in their death.

- Finding a white hair on a black cat is good luck! But it shouldn't be plucked out, or the luck will turn bad. (Some, however, say that managing to pull the single white hair out will result in a long and happy marriage!)

- Some people believe that if a funeral procession meets up with a black cat, another family member will soon die (rather gloomy!).

- Scottish myth has it that a black cat on his doorstep brings prosperity.

- Black cats crossing your path are unlucky in most parts of the world, but lucky in the UK.

● In some communities, the wives of fishermen keep their black cats indoors whilst their husbands are out at sea, in the belief that this will keep the men safe until their return.

Pocket fact ❖

Latvian farmers hope to find black kittens in their harvest. They believe that they are the spirit of a god of harvest, Rungis.

Many short stories are based around myths concerning black cats. Some of the most extraordinary (and indeed unlikely!) have been collected here.

Once upon a time in Scotland, an old farmer noticed that much of the content of his wine cellar kept disappearing. Frustrated, suspicious, and determined to catch the thieves responsible, he armed himself with a knife one night and hid behind some barrels in the cellar where the wine was stored. Lying awake in wait, he heard a rustling, and lashed out with his blade. The resulting sound was a high-pitched meow, and several black cats scuttled away into the night. Only a severed black leg remained.

The next day, the old lady next door, known to have owned a little black cat, was found bleeding to death. One of her legs had been hacked off.

A young boy was once playing on a moor alone, when, upon following a well-trodden path into a leafy enclosure he came upon a group of mysterious women chanting. They were all huddled together and seemed to be unaware of his presence. Frightened, he closed his eyes tight and turned to run back to the open area, but as he glanced backwards from the path his eyes were met with the sight of a swarm of black cats running in opposite directions.

He returned home, visibly shaken, and his mother gently coaxed him to tell her what he had seen. A few days later, he was found dead, his body covered in scratches and claw-marks.

A very different myth concerns cats of a different colour in a different country:

In Asia many years ago, and the Philippines even today, myths are passed from generation to generation about cats, a popular and useful pet. However, according to legend, male cats who are born with coats of three colours will inevitably reign as king of their territory.

Supposedly, in order to prevent the burden of being ruled by a cat who thought himself 'king', all adult cats murder three-coloured tomcats.

Pocket fact ❖

Jack Wright, of Kingston, Ontario, is the Guinness World Record holder for the biggest amount of domestic cats owned at one time: 689. A farmer in Texas is said to have kept 1,400 cats on his farm, but some of these were feral.

❧ ART ❧

Cats have been painted, sculpted and generally represented in the world of art for as long as they have been known to exist.

Pocket fact ❧

The 3,200-year-old Book of the Dead *features a spotted cat created on papyrus: it can therefore be said that drawings of cats have been around longer than paper has!*

- Egyptian sculptures and paintings depict grand and beautiful cats, in keeping with their deified status, and ever since then they have been a near-constant feature in the visual arts. Many ancient Egyptian deities were depicted as cats; the sphinx is shown as having the body of a lion with a human head; the goddess of justice and execution, Mafdet, was depicted as having the head of a lioness, and later, the cat goddess Bastet stood for fertility, protection and motherhood.

- **Steinlen:** Steinlen was one of the most famous illustrators and painters of the feline form. His instantly recognisable *Chat Noir* graces the walls of thousands upon thousands of homes all over the world, and even aside from this, his artwork is littered with cats, everywhere. Ladies out shopping carry handsome cats in their baskets, advertisements for French chocolate feature little black cats in the corner, and one painting even depicts an entire city of cats, gazing up at a full moon. Steinlen, one might say, is a master of cat art.

- **Manet:** Edouard Manet famously painted cats, and many of his paintings of them are instantly recognisable. His etching,

Les Chats, is perhaps one of his most innovative works, depicting three cats and using different techniques to portray each of them. His notebooks are full of drawings of cats in various poses, and his biographers have noted his love for the animals.

Pocket fact ❧

There is even a cat in the painting of The Last Supper, *by Ghirlandaio in 1480, and later versions of the picture also include feline subjects.*

- **Renoir:** Manet's contemporary, Auguste Renoir was also a huge fan of cats. He had many prowling around his beautiful country home in Cagnes sur Mer (near Nice), and his most famous cat painting is the aptly named *Girl with a Cat*. His cats were always depicted as happy and contented.

- **Paul Klee:** Artist Paul Klee had several cats which featured in his paintings. Mys, Nuggi, Fritzi and Bimbo all featured in author Marina Alberghini's homage to Klee's love of cats – she wrote *Il Gatto Cosmico di Paul Klee (The Cosmic Cats of Paul Klee)* and included all Klee's pets in the book.

Pocket fact ❧

The artist Andy Warhol was not known for his love of feline friends. However, two years after his death two cat books written and illustrated by Warhol in the 1950s were published, featuring sketches of his own cats Hester and Sam. Only 190 numbered copies of these books were printed exclusively for his friends.

🐾 BIG SCREEN CATS 🐾

Cats have appeared on the big screen in a large number of films over the years, whether as the stars, for example in the Disney film *The Aristocats*, or as essential plot devices. How many times have you seen someone go back to rescue their cat and become embroiled in a chain of events?

Pocket fact 🐾

Perhaps the cat that has been seen the most on the big screen is the Metro-Goldwyn-Mayer lion, who has been roaring at the beginning of films since 1924. The current lion, Leo, has been used in films for over 50 years.

Normally cats only get the starring role in children's films, mostly animated ones such as *The Aristocats* and *The Lion King*. Other notable cat movies include *That Darn Cat!*, *The Cat in the Hat* and *The Nine Lives of Thomasina*. In these films the cats are portrayed either as mischievous and lovable characters who bring a sense of fun to the world or as vital players in the unravelling of a mystery or series of events.

Orangey, a red tabby cat, is best known for his role in *Breakfast at Tiffany's* (1961) in which he played Cat, Audrey Hepburn's 'poor slob without a name'. He enjoyed a prolific career in film and television in the 1950s and early 1960s and was the only cat to win two Patsy Awards (Picture Animal Top Star of the Year, an animal actor's version of an Oscar).

Cats often appear alongside their canine counterparts in films, for example in the famous story of *Homeward Bound* or in more recent films, such as *Oliver & Company* or *Bolt*.

A relatively new famous cat is 'Don Piano', an unidentified long-haired house cat so-nicknamed by internet fans that have viewed a video clip on the website YouTube. The clip, which has been viewed over 1,000,000 times, depicts the cat making vocal sounds that are interpreted by subtitles to be a song or a poem, thought to be entitled 'Oh Long Johnson'. It's definitely worth a visit!

Cats and women

There seems to have been a special relationship between cats and women throughout the ages. Whether it is in the depiction of Egyptian goddesses or famous actresses trying their best to channel their inner feline, there is something to be said for the connection between women and cats. This was once used in a derogatory way, for example the association with witchcraft or the root of the word moggy (apparently associated with prostitution), but there is an undeniable link between cats and women stretching back though time. Some even argue that cats prefer the sound of a woman's voice.

🐈 CATS ON TELEVISION 🐈

Cats have appeared in several television shows over the years, again mostly children's cartoon programming. The most famous of these are Tom (Jerry's arch enemy), Garfield, Heathcliff, Top Cat, the Pink Panther, Tigger, Jess (from Postman Pat), Bagpuss, Sylvester and the Thundercats. Here's a rundown of our feline favourites . . .

Bagpuss: One of the most adorable famous cats to have existed, and his huge pink and cream coloured furry body is loved by generations. Made popular by the television series of the same name aired in the 1970s, only 13 episodes were ever made, yet the mark they made has lasted to this very day. Bagpuss' distinctive pink coat was actually a mistake: the company dyeing his fur were instructed to make it bright orange, creating a ginger marmalade cat, but they made a rather noticeable mistake. Peter Firmin, who created Bagpuss along with Oliver Postgate, described the mistake as the best thing that could have happened.

Garfield: created by Jim David in 1978 and named after Jim's grandfather, James Garfield Davis, Garfield is a lazy, fat, selfish tabby cat who makes life hard for his owner, Jon, and Odie the dog. His favourite food is lasagne and he hates raisins and spiders. First a comic strip, Garfield has spawned two TV series and two animated films. It currently holds the Guinness World Record for being the world's most syndicated comic strip, appearing in 2,580 newspapers and journals.

Top Cat: Born in the 1960s, Top Cat is the star of a Hanna Barbera cartoon that still airs today on channels such as Cartoon Network and Boomerang. He is a little yellow cat with a bright purple hat and vest, and is friends with everybody as well as being the leader of the gang. The cats are forever trying to make money through scams and harebrained schemes, and provide constant entertainment.

Sylvester: Sylvester and Tweety Pie, the cartoon duo that epitomise the love–hate relationship, have been on our screens since 1945. Sylvester has won three Academy Awards, and is famous for his lisp – and dying (he has 'died' in more episodes than any other Looney Tunes character). Instantly recognisable for his black and white furry form, Sylvester is somewhat sheepish, and often loses in fights against his miniature yellow bird friend. He is hugely popular, and has given his name to a massive number of pet cats worldwide.

Tom and Jerry: Tom and Jerry have been chasing each other around our screens since the early 1940s. Tom, a grey and white fluffy tomcat, relentlessly pursued his little brown mouse friend Jerry for decades, and the programme is still aired on channels such as Cartoon Network today. He emerges above all as a bit of a softy, and has the same 'lovable loser' quality that characterises Sylvester. Tom and Jerry supposedly hate each other, but there are hints throughout that they are actually friends.

The Cat in the Hat

Dr Seuss' famous creation first appeared in storybooks in 1954. His distinctive huge red and white striped hat is instantly recognisable, as is his cheeky grin and the bow-tie and umbrella that complete his jaunty look. The book is purposefully very simple, containing only 223 different words used over and over, and there are only four three-syllable words in the entire book, the rest are two or fewer. The cat has been adored by generations because of his accessibility to children, his humour and, above all, his naughtiness. He is perhaps, despite being a pencil drawing, one of the most realistic of all cartoon cats.

Cats also feature regularly in advertising or as the face of brands, most notably Felix, the Whiskas cat, the Sheba cat and Tony the Tiger. Exxon also used a tiger in their advertising, but were later sued by Kellogg's for the similarity to their mascot Tony.

The Blue Peter cats are perhaps the most famous pet cats in the UK and the show has owned nine cats since 1964. The current cats, Socks and Cookie, caused a viewer outcry after the producers falsified the results of a vote to choose the name of the new cat. The viewers chose Cookie but were given Socks, so now they have both.

Pocket fact ❀

Krazy Kat became the first cat to star in a comic strip when he appeared in the New York Journal *in 1910.*

The biggest cat phenomenon of recent years is the Japanese character Hello Kitty. This adorable white kitten was created in 1974 and now stars in a television series and several video games, adorns thousands of products in numerous shops around the world and is even the face of a maternity hospital, a credit card, an aeroplane, a restaurant and a theme park.

Pocket fact ❀

A kitten called Jazz crossed the Atlantic on the first airship flight from England to America.

❦ CATS AND MUSIC ❧

Cats have featured in a variety of songs over the years, although many don't actually mention cats in the lyrics. Here is a list of just a few:

- 'Siamese Cat Song' from *Lady and the Tramp*, by Freddie and the Dreamers

- 'The Cat in the Window' by Petula Clark

- 'The Cat Came Back' by The Muppets

- 'I Tawt I Taw a Puddy Tat' by Mel Blanc

- 'Tom Cat' by Rooftop Singers

- 'Everybody Wants to be a Cat' from *The Aristocats*

- 'Cats in the Cradle' by Harry Chapin

- 'Cat People' by David Bowie

- 'Phenomenal Cat' by The Kinks

- 'They Call Her the Cat' by Elton John

- 'Stray Cat Blues' by The Rolling Stones

- 'Leave my Kitten Alone' by The Beatles

- 'An Cat Dubh (The Black Cat)' by U2

- 'The Cats in the Well' by Bob Dylan.

Pocket fact ❧

The song 'Delilah' by Queen, was written by Freddie Mercury about his pet cat. Mercury paid tribute to Delilah, a male tortoiseshell cat, on the Queen album, Innuendo. He owned many cats throughout his life, including Tom, Jerry, Oscar, Tiffany, Goliath, Miko, Romeo, and Lily, and his solo album Mr Bad Guy is dedicated to cat-lovers all over the world.

A love of music?

There has been some research done which suggests that cats do have musical preferences. Austrian scientists found that cats preferred the oboe and male voice choirs to other types of instruments.

Rather cruelly there is an instrument dating from 1650 called a 'cat paino'. The device was made by a German scholar to entertain an Italian prince. The inventor collected cats with varying pitches to their meows and arranged them in a line according to these pitches. He would then play a 'tune' by poking the cats in the tail. Thankfully this instrument is no longer in use.

Pocket fact ❧

Cats are the only domestic animal not to be mentioned in the Bible.

Cats the musical

The musical Cats by Andrew Lloyd Webber first appeared in London's West End in 1981 and later went on to Broadway, where it ran for 18 years. The musical has toured the world and has been translated into 10 languages.

The story is based on T S Eliot's collection of poems entitled Old Possum's Book of Practical Cats, and many of the poems feature in the lyrics. The show is best known for its amazing costumes and sets, and the song Memory, now most often associated with Elaine Page.

The show features a number of memorable characters including The Old Grumbie Cat (a large tabby), Rum Tum Tugger (a wild tomcat), Mr Mistoffelees (a small black cat), Macavity (the villain of the show) and Grizabella (an old grey cat).

The musical tells the story of a group of alley cats, called the Jellice Cats, and follows them through the Jellice Ball, where they introduce themselves and the other cats who appear throughout the show.

The show has won numerous awards, including an Olivier Award for Best New Musical and a Tony Award for Best Musical.

Judi Dench was originally cast in the part of Grizabella, but she injured herself during rehearsals. Elaine Page was then cast and the song Memory was given to her.

🐈 CAT QUOTATIONS 🐈

Cats inspire philosophical musings: their relaxed attitude to the world, their refusal to do anything that displeases them, and their shameless pleasure-seeking all contribute to human admiration for them. As a result there are hundreds upon thousands of quotations relating to cats, and here some of the funniest, warmest and thought-provoking have been collected for your amusement and perusal.

'One cat just leads to another.'
Ernest Hemingway

'In ancient times, cats were worshipped as gods. They have never forgotten this.'
Terry Pratchett

'Dogs come when they're called; cats take a message and get back to you later.'
Mary Bly

'There are two means of refuge from the misery of life — music and cats.'
Albert Schweitzer

'I have studied many philosophers and many cats. The wisdom of cats is infinitely superior.'
Hippolyte Taine

'Beware of people who dislike cats.'
Irish saying

'I think all cats are wild. They only act tame if there's a
saucer of milk in it for them.'
Douglas Adams

'Perhaps God made cats so that man might have
the pleasure of fondling the tiger . . .'
Robertson Davies, *The Diary of Samuel Marchbanks*

'Way down deep, we're all motivated by the same urges.
Cats have the courage to live by them.'
Jim Davis

'When I play with my cat, who knows whether she is not
amusing herself with me more than I with her.'
Michel de Montaigne

'Women and cats will do as they please, and men and
dogs should relax and get used to the idea.'
Robert A. Heinlein

'If cats could talk, they wouldn't.'
Nan Porter

'I have noticed that what cats most appreciate in a human being is not
the ability to produce food which they take for granted — but his or her
entertainment value.'
Geoffrey Household

'Cats are rather delicate creatures and they are subject to a good many
ailments, but I never heard of one who suffered from insomnia.'
Joseph Wood Krutch

'People that hate cats will come back as mice in their next life.'
Faith Resnick

'Cats seem to go on the principle that it never does any harm to ask for what you want.'
Joseph Wood Krutch

'After scolding one's cat one looks into its face and is seized by the ugly suspicion that it understood every word. And has filed it for reference.'
Charlotte Gray

'Cats are the ultimate narcissists. You can tell this by all the time they spend on personal grooming. Dogs aren't like this; a dog's idea of personal grooming is to roll in a dead fish.'
James Goreman

'No amount of time can erase the memory of a good cat, and no amount of masking tape can ever totally remove his fur from your couch.'
Leo Dworken

'With their qualities of cleanliness, discretion, affection, patience, dignity, and courage, how many of us, I ask you, would be capable of becoming cats?'
Fernand Mery

'A meow massages the heart.'
Stuart McMillan

'If a dog jumps into your lap it is because he is fond of you; but if a cat does the same thing it is because your lap is warmer.'
A.N. Whitehead

CAT SAYINGS

Have you ever realised just how much you mention cats on a daily basis? Even those non-cat lovers amongst us are always chattering on about feisty felines, yet few of us notice just how much they feature in our day-to-day speech.

'She' is the cat's mother

According to traditional good manners, one shouldn't dismiss anyone by referring to her as 'she'. This saying probably comes from times when children were forbidden to refer to their elders or betters in this way: when they neglected to call them by name or relation, they were reminded that only distant and unimportant acquaintances could be dismissed as 'she'. The cat's mother isn't even the cat itself, and was probably worthy of very little respect.

To let the cat out of the bag

To tell a secret, or expose something that had remained hidden. The origins of the saying lie in olden times, when piglets were sold to traders in bags. In an attempt to make more money, these traders would place a large cat in the bag instead, take the money, and hope that the customer would arrive home before noticing. Hence, when the cat got out of the bag, all dishonesty was revealed.

Cat-calling

Criticising somebody's acting performance by shouting, booing and hissing from the audience. The term supposedly comes from Shakespearean times when the noises made by his audiences sounded like cats yowling and squealing.

Catwalk

This word is so common in the English vocabulary that it barely seems strange at all. Its origins do actually make a lot of sense, though: it is a long thin strip of elevated ground to be walked along, and this activity is strongly reminiscent of the balancing acts cats are so good at.

Cat's got your tongue

The explanation behind this expression, meaning that one is not speaking, often because they are afraid or shy, is rather grim. Hundreds of years ago, liars were apparently punished by having their tongues chopped out. The tongues were then fed to the King's pet cats!

Like a cat on a hot tin roof

This refers to somebody who is agitated, jumpy and nervous. This makes sense, because a cat on any hot surface will obviously be uncomfortably jumping about in an attempt to protect its paws from being burnt.

No room to swing a cat

Suggests that the space in question is very confined. Swinging cats was apparently once a very popular sport, and took many forms. Sometimes cats were swung by their tails over a rope, sometimes they were hurled at a tree . . . the horrendously cruel nature of this is the origin of the much-used proverb.

Pocket fact ❖

Folklore states that if you find a white cat sitting on your doorstep just before your wedding it is a sign of lasting happiness.

It's raining cats and dogs

This popular phrase has a variety of possible origins. Some believe that the saying relates back to Norse weather lore, when rain was equated with cats, and wind with dogs. It is also thought that the phrase could date back to medieval times when during heavy rain the corpses of cats and dogs would be washed through poor drainage systems. There is also the possibility that the phrase stems from the time when most cottages had thatched roofs, allowing animals to crawl in to take shelter, only to be washed into the house during heavy rain.

Pocket fact ❧
Cats overtook dogs as the most popular pet in America in 1987.

Pocket fact ❧
The world record for the cat with most toes beongs to Jake who has 28 toes, with 7 on each paw.

🐈 FAMOUS CAT OWNERS 🐈

Russell Brand

Russell makes no secret of his love for his cat, Morrissey. He is such a well-known ailurophile that Lindsay Lohan allegedly sent him a cat as a last-ditch attempt to get him to date her, after he repeatedly ignored her emails!

Winston Churchill

Churchill was a huge fan of cats. He owned several cats, including Nelson, a black cat that sat in a chair next to Churchill in both the Cabinet and dining rooms (named after Lord Nelson); Jock, a ginger kitten, that Churchill called his 'special assistant' and mentioned Jock in his will; Blackie, Bob, Margate (black stray) and Mr Cat also were his or his family's.

Ernest Hemingway

Hemingway had over 30 cats at one time, and took in any stray that crossed his path. He was particularly fond of polydactyls (cats with multiple toes). There are now more than 60 at the Hemingway museum in his old home, and over half of these are polydactyl.

Edgar Allan Poe

Poe's black cat Catarina inspired *The Black Cat*, and didn't leave his wife's bed as she lay dying of tuberculosis. He often portrays cats as dark and witchlike, but biographers have noted his genuine love for felines.

Alistair Darling

Sybil the cat moved in with politician Alistair and his wife in 2007, and elicited collective cooing from the nation with her first press pictures. Sybil has been given free rein in 11 Downing Street, and Darling has freely admitted his love for the furry creatures.

Justin Hawkins

Justin (lead singer of The Darkness) came out of rehab after recovering from drug addiction and became addicted to Bengal cats instead. He has three kittens named Barnaby, Troy and Cully, and claims he spends far more on their upkeep than he used to do on drugs!

Calvin Klein

Calvin Klein is apparently a huge fan of Bengal cats. When he bought his newest kittens, he flew to collect them personally in his own private jet.

Queen Victoria

The Queen is said to have been a great cat lover, and had many during her lifetime. Her favourite was called White Heather, and outlived her. White Heather was inherited by Edward VII, her son and successor to the throne.

Anne Frank

Whilst in hiding in the loft, Anne Frank's family had three cats with them, and she also writes in her diary of how she pines for the cat she had to leave behind when the family went into hiding. Her love for the animals is frequently expressed.

Pocket fact ❧

Napoleon Bonaparte, Julius Caesar and Henry II, all suffered from ailurophobia, the fear of cats.

Freddie Mercury

Freddie was a huge fan of cats, and his favourite was called Delilah. He had many throughout his lifetime, and they all had delightfully imaginative names, including: Lily, Oscar, Goliath, Tom, Jerry, Tiffany and Miko.

Marilyn Monroe

Marilyn was susceptible to feline charms, and owned several cats in the 1950s. Her favourite was a fluffy white Persian called Mitsou.

John Lennon

John Lennon had countless cats throughout his lifetime, and much has been written on his love for felines.

Pocket fact ❧

Bill Clinton's cat while he was in the White House was called Socks.

✔ CAT JOKES 🐱

Q: Where does a cat go when it loses its tail?
A: *The re-tail store.*

Q: What does a cat like to eat on a hot day?
A: *Mice cream.*

Q: What do cats use to make coffee?
A: *A purr-colator.*

Q: What do you call a cat that has swallowed a duck?
A: *A duck-filled fatty puss.*

Q: What's the difference between a cat and a comma?
A: *One has claws at the end of its paws, and the other a pause at the end of its clause!*

Q: What is a cat's favourite colour?
A: *Purrrple.*

Q: What is a cat' favourite food?
A: *Mice pudding.*

Q: Why did the cats sell their homes?
A: *The neighbourhood had gone to the dogs.*

Q: Why did the cat like to go bowling?
A: *He was an alley cat.*

Q: Where do cats like to go for days out?
A: *To a mewseum.*

Q: What would you get if you crossed a cat and a donkey?
A: *A Mewl.*

Q: What do you call a lemon-eating cat?
A: *A Sour puss!*

Q: Why don't cats play poker in the jungle?
A: *Too many cheetahs.*

Q: What do you call a cat that gets caught by the police?
A: *The purr-petrator.*

Q: How does a cat get its own way?
A: *With friendly purr-suasion.*

Q: What do you call a cat that lives in an igloo?
A: *An eskimew.*

Q: What do cats eat for breakfast?
A: *Mice Krispies.*

Q: Why are cats such good singers?
A: *Because they're very mewsical.*

Q: What is a cat's favourite magazine?
A: *Good Mousekeeping.*

Q: Where is one place that your cat can sit, but you can't?
A: *Your lap.*

Q: What kind of cat will keep your grass short?
A: *A Lawn Meower.*

Q: Why did the judge dismiss the entire jury made up of cats?
A: *Because each of them was guilty of purr-jury.*

Q: What do you use to comb a cat?
A: *A catacomb.*

Q: Why did the cat run from the tree?
A: *Because it was afraid of the bark!*

Q: Why is it so hard for a leopard to hide?
A: *Because he's always spotted.*

3

OWNING A CAT

'Everyone knows that there's no such thing as a cat owner.'
Nicholas Haworth

🐈 BEFORE YOU DECIDE TO GET 🐈 A CAT . . .

Before you rush out and buy your perfect kitten, there are a few things you should consider first.

Cost of owning a cat over its life
(average lifespan 14 years)

One 60p tin of cat food daily:	£3,066
80p box of biscuits a week:	£583
Annual insurance at £75 per year:	£1,050
Litter at £3 a week:	£2,184
Fortnight's cattery fees at £84 a time:	£1,176
One £50 sickness visit to vet each year:	£700
Routine vaccinations, flea and worm treatment:	£600
Bedding and sundry equipment:	£100
Total:	**£9,459**

CAN *YOU* KEEP A CAT?

There are several things to consider before choosing your cat. Do you have the right kind of lifestyle and the commitment it takes to own a cat?

Pocket tip

Many people choose to own a cat as they think it will be cheaper than owning a dog, but this is often not the case. Cats require frequent vaccinations and vet check-ups, so cost shouldn't be a factor in choosing a cat.

- There are other health issues that you will need to make decisions about when owning a cat, such as declawing or spaying or neutering. These are important decisions that will radically affect your cat and your lifestyle with your cat, so they shouldn't be taken lightly.

- Cats have been known to live for 20 years or more. Do you have the long-term commitment to care for a cat for its entire life? Like dogs, cats shouldn't be merely an exciting gift that is abandoned a short time later. Make sure a cat will fit in with your home and lifestyle. Cats are known to scratch furniture and many people find the amount of hair they shed very taxing to clean up (especially for long-haired breeds).

- Likewise for the cat litter box: can you handle the regular cleaning this will require? If you have children, you'll also need to make sure they will treat the cat well and try to choose a cat that won't scratch or bite them.

- If you have other pets, you will need to be sure they will get along.

Having carefully considered all of these issues, if you think that owning a cat is right for you then your next big decision is where to get your cat.

Pocket fact ❧

Owning a cat has been proven to reduce stress and lower blood pressure.

Faith, the church cat

During the Second World War, a fearless tabby cat called Faith received a PDSA Silver Medal for her bravery in caring for her kitten, Panda. A few years earlier, the stray cat had become an honorary member of St Faith and St Augustine's church (near St Paul's Cathedral). The night of the raid, the priest had tried removing the cats, but Faith returned to her safe place within the church. During the raid, many homes near the church were destroyed and more than 400 people died. The church itself was virtually destroyed, but Faith and her kitten were miraculously found safe and sound. Soon after they had been rescued, the church's roof caved in. To mark Faith's bravery, a plaque was erected in the church, part of it reading:

"On Monday, September 9th, 1940, she endured horrors and perils beyond the power of words to tell. Shielding her kitten in a sort of recess in the house (a spot she selected three days before the tragedy occurred), she sat the whole frightful night of bombing and fire, guarding her little kitten."

WHERE SHOULD YOU GET YOUR CAT FROM?

There are thousands of cats across the UK that are desperate for a new home. Choosing between cattery, pet shop, or the neighbour whose cat has just given birth to a litter of kittens can be a real challenge.

CATTERIES

Many cats are waiting patiently in catteries for the right owner to come along and rescue them. By choosing to adopt a cat from a cattery, you could be saving its life, as sadly many cats are put down after remaining unadopted for a lengthy period of time, in order to make room for new cats.

There are hundreds of catteries in the UK, mostly concentrated around big cities, notably Manchester and London. Although there are relatively few in Scotland, Wales and Ireland, adopting a rescue cat or kitten is still an option that should be considered. The website www.catchat.org/adoption has an interactive map of rescue shelters all over the UK.

Pocket tip

If you choose to go to a cattery, the procedure will probably involve quite simply walking around and seeing if any cat takes your fancy. The cats should all appear to be relatively contented and their environment should be clean and comfortable.

Tips on choosing a cat

- Most owners claim that their cat 'chose them', having fallen in love at first sight with a cat begging for a home.

- Each cat should be checked carefully before you decide to take it home, though: don't fall for the runt of a litter of kittens because it looks helpless (it will probably cost you a fortune in vet bills and may not live very long), and don't choose a visibly sickly older cat out of sympathy (for the same reasons, both financial and health-related).

- Chat to the people who look after the cats about its temperament and make sure that it fits your family. If it is known to be shy and quiet, it probably won't take well to children, but may be the perfect companion for an older person. If it is lively and fearless, take it home to your kids!

Pocket fact ❖

In ancient Rome the cat was the symbol for liberty.

ADOPTING STRAYS

> *'When a cat adopts you there is nothing to be done about it except to put up with it until the wind changes.'*
> T.S. Eliot

This tends to happen a lot. Many stray cats wander around neighbourhoods, snaffling bits of food from various friendly humans and sleeping in garden sheds. Some kind-hearted person usually takes pity on these roaming strays eventually, many of whom were once housecats but have either been kicked out or simply got lost. Regular feeding turns into regular petting, then they're allowed in the house for a bit of warmth and, *voilà*! A loving friendship is formed, a name is given, and a cat is acquired.

Despite this often happening, few people are aware of the risks of adopting a strange cat.

- Before deciding to keep a cat you don't know, take it to the vet. He or she can check it for any health problems, see whether or not it has been neutered or spayed, and even in the case of female cats check that there are no kittens on the way.

- Check for a collar and address – it may well be that you can find the owner and return the cat to its actual owner.

Pocket fact ❀

About 18% of cats in the UK were adopted after they turned up on the doorstep.

PET SHOPS

Many organisations advise against getting cats and kittens from pet shops. This is because many kittens here come from 'kitten mills', where cats are bred purely for profit and often live in terrible conditions (even employees of pet shops are often unaware of this). The cats are often overpriced, but some pet shops are battling against kitten mills and working with animal shelters, helping them to re-home their cats.

Pocket tip ✎

Ask the pet shop where they get their kittens from, and don't be afraid to check with the place they give you.

'FREE TO A GOOD HOME'

A popular way to acquire a cat is to take in a local kitten that is being given away. These cats may be found through friends, bulletin boards in supermarkets and local shops, or adverts in the newspaper. This is usually a fairly safe way of adopting a cat, as you will probably see it in its home environment and you will also have the opportunity to check that the mother cat and other kittens are healthy and well cared for.

Pocket tip

Be aware that those giving away kittens are advised to put a small price on them, not to make a profit but to ensure that the kitten is going to a safe home: free kittens could end up in the hands of any cruel stranger.

❦ WHICH CAT IS RIGHT ❧ FOR YOU?

CAT OR KITTEN? OLD OR YOUNG?

'You cannot help but smile in the company of kittens.'
Madelaine Bamford

Choosing whether to adopt a kitten or an adult cat is definitely something that should be considered carefully, and the decision relies mainly on your own circumstances.

- Kittens are the popular choice. Their crazy excitement for the world around them is endearing, and their wild antics keep owners entertained for hours on end. Bear in mind that as cute as kittens are, they demand a lot of attention. They can barely be left unsupervised, they cannot be let outside alone, and they need housetraining and toilet training . . . The happy news is that they're actually relatively easy to train if you have a little time on your hands, and are certainly less work than a puppy, or even a grown dog.

- Deciding to home an older cat has many advantages, and should not be dismissed because the prospect of a newborn kitten seems cute. Most fully grown cats are already house-trained, and their temperament is often known.

- Older cats are usually calm and relaxed companions, more interested in sitting on your lap than tearing around the house and climbing up the curtains. And advantages such as taking in a cat that can already use a litter tray speak for themselves.

Pocket tip

Kittens grow up in just six months. Your kitten may seem tiny in the cattery, but will you be prepared to deal with a fully grown cat in six months' time?

MALE OR FEMALE?

Tomcats are notoriously problematic, as unless they are neutered at five months old they will spray very strong-smelling urine (anywhere) in a bid to attract female cats for mating. Fully grown male cats can also be big and boisterous, and unless they have been spayed make impossible house cats.

That's not to say that only female cats should be kept as pets, though; if you get a male kitten, just make sure he is neutered before the age of six months and there will be no problems.

Pocket tip

It is much cheaper to neuter a male kitten than to spay a female, so a male kitten is sometimes a more attractive option: the sex makes no difference once spaying or neutering has taken place.

Females are traditionally easier to care for, mostly for the above reasons. If a female cat is not spayed, there are no really unpleasant consequences other than the odd yowl when she is in heat. Every pet cat should be spayed, though, otherwise unplanned pregnancy and unwanted kittens are a huge risk: if a female cat goes outdoors she will almost certainly become pregnant unless spayed, and it is irresponsible to neglect to take her to the vet and get the job done.

Once spayed, the sex of your cat becomes almost irrelevant. It's all about personality!

PEDIGREE OR MOGGY?

Turn to p. 25 for the advantages and disadvantages of pedigrees and moggies. The most important consideration to bear in mind is how much care you can provide your cat with: if you work full-time and plan to allow your cat outdoors for exercise, then a common British moggy is best for you, a decision taken by 97% of UK cat owners.

- Moggies are usually easy-going, undemanding and low maintenance, but they provide you with the same love and joy that any pedigree would.

- On the other hand, pedigrees tend to have predictable temperaments and short-haired breeds can be almost as easy to care for as moggies. It may be reassuring to know what you are getting.

HOW MANY CATS?

Unless you already have a whole host of pussycats prowling around the house, getting more than one at the same time can be a really good idea, especially if you're getting kittens.

This ensures that they get to know their environment in each other's company, and are more likely to get on and accept each other than if they come home separately. If this happens, the first to arrive already considers itself the boss, and conflict may ensue.

🐈 OTHER CONSIDERATIONS 🐈

- Do you already have a cat? Or any other animals? If so, it's worth considering how they will react to a new furry member of the family. Adult cats can be upset by the introduction of another cat, especially if it is a kitten that will relentlessly pounce on them and expect to play.

- Adult cats do often accept kittens more easily than fully grown cats, because they are more willing to learn and accept that they are not the boss.

- Dogs and cats have a famously volatile relationship that usually ends up in either love or hate, and the latter is a real risk.

- If choosing a pedigree, some breeds get along with other animals and children better than others (see the section on 'Breeds of Pedigree Cat' starting on p. 25) — research carefully before investing.

- If you are planning to home a common cat, the best you can do is ensure that the new cat is allowed to see other cats or dogs only for short periods of time initially under strict supervision. Increase these times, and the animals should gradually learn to tolerate each other even if they do not become friends.

Pocket fact 🐾

Born in the Vatican, the very holy cat Micetto was the pet of Pope Leo XII. He was greyish-red with black stripes and is said to have lived among the Pope's robes.

Cat and dog love

In January 2008 a dog called Arthur warmed animal-lovers' hearts by an act of grave-digging. It was so distressed at the death of its old companion, a cat called Oscar, that it retrieved the corpse from its burial spot in the garden. Oscar certainly isn't the first pet dog who has loved a cat, but it's important to remember that fairytale friendships like this need lots of hard work and wisdom. One false step, and a lifetime of work is undone.

Pocket fact ❖

The record for the longest whisker on a cat measured 19 cm (7.5 in) and belongs to Missi, a Maine Coon. The whiskers were measured in Finland on December 22, 2005.

🐈 LIFE STAGES OF A CAT 🐈

KITTENS

> *'The smallest feline is a masterpiece.'*
> Leonardo Da Vinci

Bringing your kitten home

Make sure that you have enough time on your cat's first day at home to show her where everything is, and to comfort and re-assure her. Set aside an area for her things: fill the litter tray with anti-clumping litter and place it in the corner furthest away from the door. Put food and water bowls far away from the tray, and allow her to explore.

The kitten's own area

Aside from containing all her belongings, the area should be secure and preferably have a door that prevents other animals and children from getting in and disturbing or upsetting her.

Pocket fact 🐾

Local folklore claims that a cat sleeping on all four of its paws is a sign of cold weather coming.

What to buy

Food and water bowls and a litter tray are obvious purchases, but there are also other little things that you might not think of:

- scoops, supplies of fresh cat litter and disposal bags
- safe toys to keep the kitten entertained, as it should be kept indoors for at least a fortnight

- shallow bowls for food and water

- a bed: either buy one, or simply make one out of a cardboard box; cut a side off, and fill it with soft warm blankets

- a cat carrier to bring her home in: you will also need it for her visits to the vet

- a scratching post (helps her claws, saves your furniture)

- a brush or comb, especially if your new kitten is not a shorthair

The first six months

These are so important in any kitten's development, and after the first 12 weeks with the mother cat, the work is up to you. You need to stroke and handle your kitten a lot to make sure that she doesn't grow up to be scared of humans. Reward all good behaviour with calm stroking and soft, gentle praise.

Pocket tip

Never shout to reprimand naughty behaviour; instead, speak firmly and walk away — your kitten will soon learn what you want (and how to get fuss!).

After six months

Things get a little easier with time, but your (almost grown-up) cat still needs attention. As she ventures outdoors and begins to do all of the things that adult cats do, you need to get her spayed (or neutered if it's a tomcat), and make sure that she has had all the vaccinations she needs. Ask your vet for advice, and make sure that you do everything he or she advises.

Pocket tip 🧶
Be careful! But allow freedom
Kittens, like children, learn by exploring. Make sure you allow them to do so, but try and keep their environment as safe as possible: no open windows, no hot rings on the cooker left on, no open doors (until your kitten is ready), no boisterous children, no poisonous plants.

TEENAGE CATS

When is a cat a 'teenager'?
Your cat will be a teenager between the ages of 8 and 12 months.

How are teenage cats different?
They are going through the transition from kitten to cat, and show traits of both. They probably aren't aware of any differences, but you might be. Your 'catten' may be tearing around the house wildly one minute, then collapse exhausted the next, falling asleep immediately. They are more likely to lash out at you, and biting and scratching are more common during this period than at any other time.

Why do teenage cats behave as they do?
Teenage cats are just like teenage humans: they are pushing the boundaries and testing you one last time before they become adults. Try to play with it and encourage activity – it can be a tiring period for owners, but rest assured, it shouldn't last more than six months. You'll then have a relatively sensible, fully grown cat.

OLDER CATS

How old is an 'older' cat?

Nowadays, cats are living so healthily and for so long that 9–10 years is only really considered to be 'middle-aged'. Anything older than this is generally regarded as 'elderly'.

How is an older cat different from the average adult cat?

Older cats are much calmer and need less careful supervision; they are much more likely to take a catnap all day long than destroy your furniture or tear around the house crazily, destroying everything in their paths.

Advantages of living with an older cat

Aside from an undamaged home, older cats have other advantages over kittens. They are already housetrained, less likely to go mousing (and leave 'presents' on the doorstep), and seek nothing more than gentle and friendly companionship from you.

Normal signs of ageing

Cats, like humans, grow frail with old age. You may notice your cat becoming thinner as well as less active, and dark fur may show a few grey hairs.

Looking after an older cat

Older cats, like older humans, are at a higher risk of becoming unwell, and may need extra vigilant attention to ensure that they stay healthy. Look out for the following:

Pocket tip
A moggy from Texas called Dusty gave birth to 420 kittens in her lifetime.

- apparent blindness or deafness

- panting even when still

- confusion

- unusual behaviour

- mobility problems beyond usual slow movement

- rashes or lumps on the skin (check with a comb)

- fast heartbeat even when not exercising

- lack of appetite

- weight loss (beyond losing a little with old age)

- vomiting that is unexplained or frequent (or both)

- problems with passing faeces

- urination problems

- dental problems

- soiling the house

- wounds and injuries

- suggestions of poisoning

- collapse or unstable walking

- withdrawn attitude

- pain

- drastic change in activity level (either becoming very lethargic in a short space of time, or becoming hyperactive for no apparent reason).

What to do if your cat seems unwell

The answer to this is really quite simple: *take it to the vet*. It isn't worth worrying about whether your cat is really ill or not, whether you're overreacting, or whether you might waste the vet's time; all vets would rather catch a problem in time than have to break it to you that it is too late.

Dealing with bereavement

No matter how well you care for your cat, the sad day will inevitably come when it is just too old to carry on. More and more people are gradually coming to realise that losing a pet can be as painful as losing a member of the family; indeed, they are a member of the family. There are now many books available on the topic, and doctors even offer counselling services akin to those offered when loved ones die.

Putting your cat to sleep

Your vet will recommend whether or not this step is necessary, but sometimes it really is the kindest thing you can do for your cat if she is in pain and unhappy.

♦ HEALTH ♦

FLEAS

Fleas are a problem that most cat owners will have to face at some point and, as grim as that may sound, there are fairly easy ways to detect and deal with the problem.

Fleas feed on the blood of the host and, as they suck this out, their saliva is simultaneously injected; this is what causes a reaction in the skin and leads to lumps, bumps and itching. They are also carriers of a kind of tapeworm, which can be deterred by regular worming.

Pocket fact ❧

If a small cat has a large flea infestation, she may lose such a huge amount of bodily fluids that she becomes dehydrated, so make sure you offer her lots of water.

Detecting fleas

- Use a fine-toothed flea comb and comb your cat over a white sheet. If any black specks appear on the sheet, it is likely that your cat has fleas. But the little bits that appear on the sheet are not the fleas themselves, rather the excess blood sucked from your cat.

- Sometimes, if the infestation has gone far enough, the white sheet treatment won't even be necessary; a little peek through her fur will provide you with an answer.

- Give your cat a bath. As you wet areas of her body, fleas will run en masse to the dry bits. So, for example, if you avoid wetting her head you will see them all run to that area.

- Watch out for scratching. It may sound obvious, and it is, but if your cat won't stop scratching, then get her on a white sheet pronto!

- The best areas to check are under the chin, behind the ears, inside the legs and at the base of the tail, and on the belly. Try and turn it into a petting session; if you make a fuss of your cat she's much less likely to notice the prodding and probing.

Pocket tip

Before treating your cat, you need to make sure that she doesn't have a flea allergy; this is possible if she has hair loss, crusty skin, or even erosions of the skin. If you think your cat may be allergic, take her to the vet rather than attempt to treat her yourself. The vet may recommend a variety of treatments, including antibiotics, ointments, antihistamines, corticosteroids or skin oil replacement treatment.

Treating fleas

- Over-the-counter treatments are available from your vet and most pet shops: invest.

- Remember that fleas don't just choose one pet to irritate. They will live anywhere and everywhere, not only on any animal but in any dark corner, any carpet, any sofa . . . not to mention cat baskets and bedding. This grim reality means that as soon as you spot any sign of one little flea, you need to act.

- Treat every animal in the house, not just the one displaying symptoms. Dogs and cats are often infected by the same kind of flea, so be vigilant, keep an eye out and treat all your animals just in case.

- Treat furniture, carpets and surroundings. Hoover vigorously, reach every little corner and don't miss a spot. Wash all pet bedding and fabrics thoroughly and buy the special flea sprays available to make sure that all of the little pests are killed and can't return.

- Repeat this procedure (a little less vigorously) about once every month or so. Try to keep the house as clean as possible anyway, and always keep an eye out for fleas returning.

Pocket tip

Remember, it's not so much about treatment as prevention. Once fleas have paid your cat a visit once, you need to be aware of the steps to take to ensure there are no further itchy outbreaks.

- *Don't wait until there are symptoms of itchiness and scratching before taking action.*
- *There are many 'once a month' products for cats and dogs that are intended for this very purpose: make the most of them, and use them religiously.*
- *Flea collars are a good idea – their success rate isn't 100%, but they have been proven to help prevention. Make sure it doesn't get wet, and check regularly for irritation: some cats may react badly to the chemicals.*

ESSENTIAL GROOMING AND MAINTENANCE

Cats need little attention compared with some other pets, but there are some things that must be done regularly to keep your cat healthy.

Pocket tip 🧶

You should NEVER trim your cat's whiskers. This can be painful and cause them to be disorientated for the two to three months it takes for their whiskers to grow back.

Grooming

Grooming may initially be a difficult or undesirable task, but there are ways around this.

- Introduce grooming gradually, and make sure the sessions are really short to start with; once she gets used to the idea, you can do a more thorough job.

- Start the routine on areas where your cat likes to be stroked and gradually move across her body, praising constantly and speaking softly and gently.

- Reassure her, and reward her with treats once the ordeal is over.

- You'll need to spend more time on longhaired cats; shorthairs only need it about once a week.

- You only need to groom your cat for about five minutes each time, and this way you'll ensure she's got a glistening coat.

Pocket tip 🧶

Long-haired cats need to be groomed every single day. This may seem like a big responsibility, but it is essential and will save both you and your cat a lot of trouble and strife in the long run. Attempting to bath fluffy cats and comb matted fur out is no joke, and won't be a pleasant experience for either of you, so invest in a comb and make it a quick five-minute part of your daily routine. Short-haired cats also need attention, although not as much.

Claw-clipping

Cats that regularly go outdoors won't need their claws clipped. You should keep an eye on them just in case, but in general, they will file their own claws down on bark and walls.

If your cat is not an outdoor cat and doesn't tend to use a scratching post (or your furniture . . .), then her claws will need clipping. This isn't an easy task, but use the same calming body language as you would for grooming, and just try to get it done as quickly and cleanly as possible.

Always avoid the pink 'quick' and leave some of her claw, otherwise you will cause her a lot of pain (and significantly reduce the possibility of claw-clipping ever taking place again).

Ear mites

These don't cause huge amounts of pain, but can irritate your cat without her even displaying any symptoms. If left untreated they can block the ear canal and cause infection, so keep an eye out. Go to the vet; they may give you treatment.

Worming

Ask your vet for advice on worming tablets, rather than just buying some from the pet shop. Cats should be treated for tapeworms and roundworms regularly, as they pose a risk not only to animals but to humans too. Symptoms are few and far between, so as potentially time-wasting and expensive as worming may seem, it is actually essential.

Pocket fact ❧

Twelve people every year in the UK suffer eye damage as a result of a roundworm infection. This happens when the eggs laid by the creatures grow and develop into larvae, making their way to the back of the eye.

General vigilance

Keep an eye on your cat's physical appearance, and get any lumps, bumps, strange markings, infections and the like checked out. Dark marks on the nose and ears could be a symptom of cancer, and infections may require antibiotics.

Cleaning by the professionals

Your cat will groom itself every day and cats are known for their general hygiene, but it can sometimes be helpful to take them to a professional groomer.

While most professional services cater more to dogs, there are several 'treatments' available for cats, such as teeth cleaning, bathing, hair clipping and shaving, nail trimming and ear cleaning.

Most salons also sell specialist products to help you look after your kitty at home. Some professionals will even come to your home to groom your pet.

Pocket fact ❧

The largest (surviving) litter of 14 kittens were born to a Persian cat called Bluebell in South Africa.

NEUTERING AND SPAYING

Generally speaking, male cats really need to be neutered at five months of age, otherwise you will not be able to keep them indoors.

- Neutering a male kitten costs between £30 and £50, and the same cost applies to females, although they may be towards the higher end of the scale. This really is a small price to pay to avoid unwanted litters, the cost of caring for them, and the stress of attempting to find homes for kittens.

- Both neutering and spaying are safe, easy and harmless procedures. Vets carry out the operations hundreds of times every month, and risk is low.

Human cat allergies

Cat allergies are not caused by a reaction to fur, which is what most people believe. It's actually to do with a secretion from the cat's sebaceous glands.

Symptoms of a cat allergy are familiar to most people who have been confronted with a wheezing, sneezing visitor. The most common indicators of an allergy include coughing and spluttering, tightening of the airways, itchy or red eyes that water, nasal congestion and itching all over.

The best way to avoid them is simply to avoid living with a cat, but this isn't always possible.

There are ways to minimise suffering if living with a cat is unavoidable. Try the following:

- *Spend as little time as possible with the cat*
- *Wash your hands often, and avoid touching your face, eyes, and any other sensitive areas.*
- *Try to have as few soft furnishings as possible, as these collect allergens.*
- *Ban the cat from as many rooms as possible, within reason (for example, don't let her snuggle up under the duvet).*
- *Reduce reactions by being sensible and basically doing everything possible to minimise contact.*

Injections actually exist to reduce reactions to cats. This is carried out periodically, and works by encouraging the body's natural immune responses to react and lessen the symptoms of the allergy. The treatment doesn't tend to have a 100% success rate, but has really helped some sufferers.

MOST COMMON CAT ILLNESSES AND THEIR SYMPTOMS

Some of the most common illnesses experienced by cats include the following:

- urinary tract infections
- gastritis/vomiting
- chronic renal failure
- enteritis and diarrhoea
- diabetes

- skin allergies
- constipation
- ear problems
- respiratory problems.

All of the above require veterinary attention, and some are more serious than others.

Other common illnesses include feline chlamydia, dry nose illness and cat flu. Your vet will be the best source of information in any emergency.

Symptoms of all of the above can vary, but any instances of your cat appearing to be lethargic or generally under the weather should be checked out immediately.

The best advice on your cat's health is to learn their habits and regular behaviour, and act immediately if anything changes. A newfound desire to sleep all day when your cat is usually an active outdoor feline may indicate that something is amiss.

Pocket fact ❖
Paracetamol is lethal for cats. The tiniest little bit of an ordinary tablet can be enough to make your cat very ill and could even kill it.

Signs a cat is ill

Vomiting and diarrhoea
Both of these can indicate something as serious as salmonella or toxic poisoning. Excessive vomiting or diarrhoea can cause further

problems such as dehydration or hypoglycaemia, which in turn may lead to fits and seizures that could even result in death. Blood in either vomit or stools means your cat needs immediate attention, as she may have ingested a mouse or rat that has been poisoned, amongst other things. This situation is fairly common, so you should be aware of the dangers.

Personality change
Know your cat well enough to notice immediately if her personality quickly becomes very different. This is especially significant if she is usually cuddly and playful but suddenly becomes withdrawn.

Lethargy
This is probably the most common sign of illness in cats. The causes for a cat being lethargic might include dehydration, infection, internal bleeding or anaemia.

Coughing and sneezing
Cats, unlike humans, don't tend to cough and sneeze very much. This means that when they do there is probably something wrong, especially as neither cats nor dogs get a 'cold' the way humans do. Coughing and sneezing will probably be the result of an upper respiratory infection, which will not heal without help from the vet. The odd sneeze is nothing to panic about and could be dust in the environment or any number of things, but if it persists, seek help.

Eating and drinking
Again, as with humans, loss of appetite usually indicates that something is amiss. If something is really wrong, she may stop eating and drinking completely, which should result in you taking her straight to the vet. Problems such as dehydration and hypoglycaemia can set in after just a few hours, so be careful.

Temperature
Your vet will tell you whether it's necessary for you to take your cat's temperature, or whether he will do this. A cat's temperature should be between 100.5°F and 102.5°F, so check that all is in order. This should be done rectally, and it's best for two of you to take on the challenge. One of you should hold the cat firmly but gently by the scruff of the neck and front legs, whilst the other inserts a thermometer (either mercury or digital) into the rectum. Remember to lubricate it well with a water-based lubricant such as KY Jelly first. The cat certainly won't enjoy the experience, but be as gentle as possible and you should get a good indicator of whether or not she is in good health.

Gums
They should be pink. Check what they usually look like when your cats is healthy so that you will be aware if something is wrong, especially as every cat is different and what is normal for one cat may be worrying in the case of another. Some colours indicate serious illness in all cats, though: these are brick red, very pale, blue, yellow and grey. One word: vet.

Dribbling, shivering and disrupted breathing
Dribbling is okay if your cat is asleep or pawing you, when it is a sign of affection (stemming from the time when she was inside her mother's womb and did so to stimulate milk flow). However, if she's shivering and breathing irregularly, too, then there may well be something wrong. They are all clear signs of great discomfort and probably pain.

Not using her litter tray
If you find little puddles or piles around the house, don't get cross with your cat, as difficult as this may seem. There will always be a reason for soiling carpets and furnishings, and it may well be that

your cat is ill. It can be a behavioural problem, caused by upsetting circumstances or big changes in the cat's life, but may also indicate a urinary infection.

Pocket tip 🧶

In all cases above, take your cat to the vet.

THE VET

Frequency of visits

If your cat seems healthy, it isn't really necessary to take her to the vet very often. You really can't blame cats for hating those visits.

- Kittens should be seen a minimum of three times during the first year of their lives, at the ages of 8 weeks, 12 weeks and 16 weeks.

- After this, presuming all vaccinations have been administered and the kitten has been either neutered or spayed, visits need not be so frequent.

How to choose your vet

- Don't just go for the vet who lives closest to you. Your vet will probably be with you throughout your cat's life, so make sure that you're happy with him or her right from the beginning.

- Ask around: your friends and neighbours with cats or other animals will have already had experiences with various veterinary practices, and may be able to either recommend or warn against vets they have encountered.

- Check out the practice yourself. There's nothing wrong with visiting a few before you sign your cat up to one place, and you can tell a lot about the place just by looking around.

- Ask about the RCVS Practice Standards Scheme. This accredits veterinary practices according to the services they provide and specialities offered. Each practice has been thoroughly checked, and participating practices have volunteered to undergo vigorous checks every few years. These are carried out by qualified inspectors, many of whom also carry out spot checks.

- Ask about costs, and check these against as many different sources as possible to make sure that they are reasonable (eg other local practices and prices online for vets in other areas, but do bear in mind that some areas are simply more expensive to live in than others).

How to deal with vet visits

Most cats hate visiting the vet. Here are some useful tips to make your preparation and visit as smooth as possible. Some cats won't even be fussed about going: they may even enjoy the extra attention.

Your behaviour

- It is essential that you are calm and relaxed – your cat will sense it immediately if you aren't, and this will add to her stress and worry.

- Keep your voice calm, soft and soothing, and talk to her all the time, from the moment you persuade her to get into her cat carrier to arrival and waiting in the surgery, and her experience on the table.

- Stroke her whenever you can, and just make sure she knows you're there. Careful with the physical contact, though – she may be agitated and not want to be stroked; try to understand if she lashes out and stop touching her.

TRAVELLING

Cat carriers

The first battle will probably be getting her into the cat carrier, which cats notoriously hate.

- Leave the carrier out in an area where she plays or sleeps all of the time.

- Put some soft blankets in it and maybe a toy.

- Do this a little while before a planned vet trip, so the carrier at least won't be a foreign, threatening object, and can even help to comfort her if she's recently been sleeping or playing in it.

Pocket tip 🐾

Choose a lightweight carrier that you can carry relatively easily. Lightweight plastic or fibreglass is best, as wire or metal ones can pose danger (eg collars catching), and they are also cold and unwelcoming. Likewise, wicker carriers may look pretty but they are usually draughty and quite difficult to clean.

- Start by placing treats inside the carrier (eg cooked chicken or catnip) to lure the cat inside. Some people even place the cat's meals inside to encourage good associations: whether or not you choose to do this is a personal decision, but the more used to the carrier your cat is, the easier it will be to get her inside on vet day.

- Cajole her gently inside. Be kind and gentle, but also firm: you don't want to prolong the ordeal or risk her running away to hide.

- If you're in a hurry and don't have time to spend on cajoling, then the easiest way to get your cat in the carrier is to turn it so that the lid is on top, pick her up, and put her inside, closing the door quickly before she has time to escape. This is also a good last-ditch attempt if all else fails. It isn't cruel: she probably won't like it, admittedly, but at least it gets the job done quickly and simply.

Pocket tip 🧶

While putting your cat in its carrier, be prepared to get clawed a bit in the process — a long-sleeved top is a good idea.

Bus and car journeys

- Don't feed or water your cat for at least an hour before the journey (to stop her from being sick).

- If you're in the car, strap the carrier in with a seatbelt.

- If on the bus, hold it tight – don't just dump your cat in the luggage area.

Pocket tip 🧶

Go on very short 'practice' drives before the trip to the vet. Make them five minutes or so in length, then gradually increase it, rewarding her with treats every time.

- Have the car window open; all travel sickness is helped by fresh air.

- Drive slowly, too; 70mph won't do anybody any favours.

Pocket fact ❧

Only 1% of cats travel contentedly; the other 99% display signs of agitation, from yowling to vomiting. Not very encouraging, but at least you can prepare . . .

- Be equipped. Take loo roll, wipes, spare towels, spare blankets, bin liners, cleaning sprays, rubber gloves . . . if you're prepared for the worst it might not even happen.

- Motion sickness tablets can be a good idea – ask your vet to recommend some (probably before you get there is a good idea).

- Bring toys, and make sure the car isn't too hot.

Pocket tip ❧

Once you and your cat return home, expect her to run away from you, straight outside usually. This is totally normal and she'll return in time – probably when it's time for dinner.

CAT FIRST AID

Firstly, just note that if you're in any doubt, get that carrier out and take your cat to the vet. Injuries and illnesses just aren't worth the risk. You may be very loving and gentle, but if you aren't qualified you can't do the job.

Pocket tip 🧶

*Phone before you go to the vet, even if it's an emergency.
Knowing you're on the way can help them to prepare, especially
if you can let them know symptoms and signs.*

Wounds

Keeping your cat in at night can prevent a lot of accidents, and
is much better than any first aid you can give. Most accidents
happen in the dark, and it's usually pretty obvious what has
happened.

- Your cat will be in great distress, and probably have very
  visible and obvious injuries, usually to the head or tail end. She
  may also be panting rapidly and have pale gums.

- Wrap her in a blanket very carefully and gently, and go to the
  vet immediately – if it's the middle of the night she may wake
  you by yowling. Call the emergency number.

- You can try to clean wounds with warm water and cotton
  wool, but be very gentle and careful. Apply direct pressure to
  wounds with a bandage, but again, be careful.

Drowning

This sounds absurd, but a drowned cat can actually sometimes be
brought back to life by mouth-to-mouth resuscitation. An older
cat or a kitten can fall into a pond and be unable to get out, and
once rescued you can help.

- Close the cat's mouth, and gently purse your lips and blow air
  into her nostrils.

- Between puffs, allow air to escape the nostrils by moving your mouth away.

If it's working, you should see your cat's chest rising and falling, and she may begin to breathe independently again.

Burns

Treat burns in much the same way as you would on a human (apart from the obvious 'get to the vet' bit).

- Get cold water on the area as quickly as possible, and follow this with a cold compress (you can niftily create one out of a bag of frozen peas and a cold, wet tea towel if you have nothing else to hand).

- The key to this is *hold it there*, for as long as you possibly can.

- If at all possible, get somebody to accompany you both to the vet and hold the compress in place throughout the journey.

Pocket fact ❧

In Buenos Aires in the 1940s a black cat called Mincha climbed a 40 foot tree and didn't come down for six years. She had three litters of kittens while living in the tree and local people fed her by putting food on poles.

PET INSURANCE

Obvious question: Is it worth it?

Answer: Yes.

It's all very well in these credit-crunch times to scrimp and save wherever possible, but your cat's health really isn't a good place to start (or indeed end). Investing just a little bit every month in pet insurance shouldn't hurt too much, although it does of course depend on your financial circumstances.

Still, if and when the time comes when your cat needs a major operation, whether it's after a car accident or a collapsed lung, you will be eternally grateful that you stowed away that little bit just in case . . . the task of breaking the news to children that their beloved cat might die because it can't have the operation it needs is a heartbreaking one that no parent wants to face (incidentally, if it does come to that, a little white lie won't hurt anybody, and money talk needn't come into it).

- Shop around for the best deal, and check what is covered. It is offered by just about everybody, and you can even pop it in your shopping basket at the supermarket (any supermarket!). A quick glance at what's available is reassuring: there is lots of competition between providers, and there are lots of good deals as a result.

- Cat insurance starts at as little as £5 a month, and covers many things. Obviously, money towards vet bills is included, but there are other benefits too, like money to offer as a reward if your cat goes missing, boarding fees and even death benefits.

Pocket tip 🧶
Even the lowest insurance packages offer respectable benefits, but it is worth getting something slightly more expensive, say for an older cat, in case vets' bills escalate and exceed the price covered by cheap packages.

- When calculating insurance prices, insurers generally just want to know the breed and age of your cat, and where you live. It's a good idea to go on price comparison websites to make sure that you get the best deal and find the package that suits you and your cat best. If you have more than one cat, there are some-times discounts offered for insuring them all with one provider.

VACCINATIONS AND INJECTIONS

There are four really essential vaccinations recommended by the Cats' Protection League. These should be carried out when kittens are 12 months old, then followed up with booster jabs when they reach a year old:

- Feline Infectious Enteritis

- Cat Flu

- Feline Leukaemia Virus

- Feline Chlamydophilosis.

Make sure you keep all records of vaccinations (usually vaccina-tion cards) — you will need them if you decide to leave your cat in a cattery at any time. If your cat is a pedigree, you will probably also need them when showing.

Pocket tip

Don't forget to give your cat regular worming tablets and treat them for fleas too. This is every bit as important as all those jabs.

HOW TO ADMINISTER TABLETS YOURSELF

If you have to give your cat tablets, there are several tricks you can use to make sure they take them. These can include:

- crushing the tablets into their food

- hiding them in fishy treats, such as tinned tuna or mackerel

- putting the cat in your lap and holding them by the scruff, then putting the tablet as far into their mouth as you can manage. Don't try this if you're worried about hurting them in any way

- buying specialist cat treats designed to hide tablets

- crushing the tablet in cream cheese and wiping it on the cat's foreleg. It will lick it off without realising.

One of the easiest ways to get a cat to take their tablets is to ask your vet for a pill pusher, which is a bit like a syringe. Filling this with water can make sure your cat will swallow the pill. You should also try stroking the cat's throat to encourage them to swallow and make sure you give them a treat afterwards!

Pocket tip 🧶
Once you have given your cat the tablet, keep an eye out to make sure it doesn't spit it out later.

Hairballs

Hairballs are a somewhat grim reality for all cat owners, but they're really nothing to worry about.

Hairballs occur because cats wash themselves with their tongues. Hair collects in the stomach over time, and eventually the cat vomits them up, occasionally along with undigested food or actual vomit.

There are some things you can do to help prevent them:

- Brush your cat regularly; then there will be much less loose hair for her to ingest.
- You could also give her 2–3 tablespoons of butter a week, which helps to loosen old hairs.
- If your cat seems to be suffering, you can give her special anti-hairball medicine and supplements. Available from your vet, these substances are 'slippery', and work towards softening hairballs, making them much easier to pass. Be careful, though, because some of these supplements contain mineral oil which, in excess quantities, is known to have an adverse effect on the amount of vitamin A in the body. Check with your vet.

How do you know if your cat is suffering?

- Look out for dry hacking and coughing, especially if it happens often, and it happens after meals.
- You may also notice that your cat's faeces is very hard and has bits of hair in it, or she may be constipated.
- Her usually silky coat might be dry and matted, and she may not want to eat, appearing slow, depressed and lethargic.
- The main sign will be the hairy lumps left on the floor . . .

🐾 FOOD AND NUTRITION 🐾

'Even overweight cats instinctively know the cardinal rule:
when fat, arrange yourself in slim poses.'
John Weitz

WHAT SHOULD YOU FEED YOUR CAT?

Food can make differences in every aspect of a cat's life: from health and the immune system to how long they actually live. It's therefore essential that you feed your cat the right things.

Dry or tinned food?

Both have their advantages, but a cat shouldn't be expected to survive on either without the other. Both dry and tinned cat food should be combined with the occasional fresh treat to ensure that your cat is healthy and stays in good shape.

Pocket fact 🐾
Cats need at least 50% of their diet to be canned or fresh food, as opposed to dry biscuits. If they don't get this, they are at risk of problems such as bladder and kidney disease, as the kidneys may become overworked.

Dry food

This is widely available, relatively cheap, and a popular choice with many cat owners. It's also perfectly okay, as long as it is accompanied with plenty of water, and your cat also has fresh food every now and then. If you feed your cat dry food exclusively, it is not only boring for her, but she will start to suffer health problems. Although it does contain the meats, fats and proteins essential to her diet, it is also full of rice and grains. These are used to bulk it out, but cats really weren't born to eat rice, and whilst it won't do them any harm at all, it won't do them much good either.

Pocket tip 🧶

Crunching on the little biscuits is really good for your cat's teeth, keeping them clean, and helping to avoid build-up of wet foods on the gums. Cats who are fed a wet-food-only diet often suffer with teeth problems, especially if their owners are unaware that they need assistance with their oral hygiene.

Wet food

- Wet food tends to be about 75% moisture, and comes in tins and foil pouches. The high moisture content is the biggest advantage talked up by vets and experts.

- If a more costly brand of food with a high meat content is chosen, then the level of nutrients is likely to be quite high. As long as the occasional bit of dry food is given to clean your cat's teeth, all should be fine.

- Do beware, though: cheap canned food can be full of 'fillers', and be quite high in salt and fat with very few nutrients.

Pocket tip 🧶

Beware of tinned cat foods that are very high in fish, as despite popular knowledge that cats love fish, it is actually quite bad for them. Too much fish can lead to 'yellow fat disease', caused by the high levels of unsaturated fatty acids.

Symptoms include abdominal pain, lethargy, fever, loss of appetite. Cats that eat a lot of red tuna are especially prone to the disease.

Homemade food

Homemade cat food can contain more nutrients and be better for your cat than shop-bought products – if you do your research. Manufactured foods have usually been carefully created to contain everything needed in a cat's diet, so owners who believe, for example, that feeding their cat nothing but fresh mice (ie feeder mice intended for snakes) is healthy, are mistaken. You can't just throw a freshly cooked chicken or fish at your cat and think you're doing her the world of good: she needs more.

- Make sure that she has the odd biscuit to crunch on, and combine both raw and cooked meat with vegetables and very small bits of bone.

- This should all be combined with plenty of vitamin supplements and also taurine (part of bile usually found in the lower intestine but available to buy as a supplement).

Pocket fact 🐾

If fed a vegetarian diet, cats will go blind, amongst other ailments.

WHEN SHOULD YOU FEED YOUR CAT?

Many cat owners argue over whether or not a responsible owner leaves food out all day or feeds at regular intervals.

The answer depends on the individual, but the basic guideline to follow is the size of your cat: if she has a constant supply of dry food to crunch on and is eating three tins of canned food a day, she is probably overweight and desperately in need of a diet.

- Cats will usually eat at the schedule you set, so if you feed them daily at 8:00am, and 6:00pm, that's when they'll expect food and act hungry.

- Three small wet meals a day is a good rule (three is the maximum, though, and make sure the portions really are small).

- Owners who are out at work are fine to feed their cat two larger meals a day.

- Leave dry food out during the day while you're out.

- Make sure she always has plenty of fresh water (very important).

- Kittens need feeding little and often, unlike fully grown cats. They obviously require that little bit extra in terms of care, so think carefully before getting one if you work all day. Like babies, their tummies are really small, so can't handle much food in one sitting. They need feeding every few hours: the best way to judge with kittens is by their own hunger. If they want it, they'll eat it. Simple.

What is actually in cat food?

Labelling laws are actually pretty lax, and what you read may not relate entirely to what is actually inside. Cheap brands are full of fillers, and usually contain a lot of carbohydrates and 'meal' to bulk out the contents. This filler usually exists in the form of corn, which is bad news for your cat. Cats tend to find corn quite difficult to digest, which in turn leads to allergies that can cause real discomfort.

In the case of dry food, these dry ingredients are actually necessary to shape the little biscuits. New processes are being developed now in more expensive brands to make this less essential, but it exists in most cat foods.

- *Look at the name of the food: foods that contain less than 95% chicken, for example, are legally not allowed to be called 'chicken cat food'. If there's 25% chicken or more, then anything along the lines of 'chicken feast' or 'chicken cat dinner' is fine, and you can be confident that there are actually some real pieces of chicken in the tin.*
- *Beware the word 'with', though. Only 3% of meat is needed for the tin to merit saying 'cat food with chicken', yet you're probably feeding your cat 97% who knows what.*
- *'Chicken flavour' means nothing at all. That tin could well be 0% chicken, and most cat owners are none the wiser.*

WHAT CATS CAN'T AND SHOULDN'T EAT

Milk

This may seem strange, given the age-old image of a cat being at her happiest when contentedly lapping a saucer of milk, but it really isn't very good for them. Don't worry, it's not toxic like chocolate, but the average well-nourished cat doesn't need it provided her diet is well balanced. Many cats are actually lactose intolerant, meaning that when they do drink milk they often get stomach upsets, cramps and wind. It is okay to treat your cat with milk sometimes, though, if she seems to really love it. Just make sure that it has a high fat content; the creamier the better (more fat means less lactose). Moderation is the key!

Onions

Onions, and even substances containing onions, are very harmful to cats. This includes things that may never cross your mind, like gravy powder, and even other related root vegetables (for example, garlic). The reason behind this is that they contain a substance called N-propyl disulphide, which causes a form of anaemia.

Chocolate

It has long been known that chocolate is toxic for dogs, but few people realise it can actually do quite a lot of damage to cats too, for much the same reason. The substance in chocolate that hurts animals so much is called theobromine, and this causes chocolate toxicity. It comes from the cocoa bean in chocolate, and signs that your cat has ingested it emerge within 24 hours. These include shaking and shivering, vomiting, diarrhoea, seizures, muscle spasms, excessive thirst and/or urination. In rare cases, chocolate toxicity can cause comas and even death because the heart beats so fast, but this really doesn't happen very often.

Pocket tip

If you suspect your cat has eaten chocolate, take her straight to the vet; don't wait for symptoms to appear.

Raw potatoes and raw tomatoes

If potatoes or tomatoes are still green, it means that your cat really shouldn't eat them (this includes green tomatoes). The leaves and stems are the most dangerous, and this is because they have the highest level of the bitter alkaloid found throughout the fruit called glycoalkaloid solanine, which will really upset your cat's stomach and cause violent vomiting and diarrhoea.

Others

Cats should avoid greens in general, along with berries, seeds and tobacco. All of these can have adverse affects, and really are best kept far out of your cat's reach (ie in a cupboard, as we all know putting things up high is no obstacle for the average pussycat).

Pocket fact ❖

Before what is now the classic British cuppa was introduced into the UK, catnip tea was the most widely consumed beverage in the country. It is also known to have herbal healing properties for humans, but doesn't have the same crazy effect as it does on cats.

Catnip

Cats go utterly crazy over catnip, yet nobody seems to really know quite what it is or quite what it does. How can a little toy bought for 99p in a pet shop elicit such excitement, just because it 'contains catnip'?

What is catnip?

It's not quite as mystical as it seems. Catnip is, quite simply, a plant; it resembles and is often mistaken for mint (which is

why it is sometimes referred to as 'catmint'). The plants are
usually about 50cm–100cm tall, and have greeny-grey
leaves and white flowers. If you look closely, you'll see that the
flowers have tiny purple spots on them. They don't grow in
the UK, though, and are more likely to be seen in the
Mediterranean countries, and more recently in the United
States.

What does catnip do?

Without beating around the bush here, it drives your cat
crazy. One sniff and your cat will paw it, lick it, roll over, rub
up against it, chew it . . . basically it can't get enough. The
reaction doesn't last very long (about five minutes), and once
your cat has reacted it won't do so again for another hour
or so. Experts have recognised that the strong reaction is
psychosexual, meaning that kittens don't react because they
aren't sexually mature.

Is it dangerous?

In a word, no. Understandably, many cat owners worry about
a substance that completely changes the behaviour of their cat,
and apparently has the same effects as many harmful drugs
have on humans. Happily, though, catnip does no harm at
all (although some cats have allergic reactions. If this happens
to your cat the solution is simple; don't give her any more
catnip). In most cats, it acts almost as an aphrodisiac would.
Despite your cat's apparently out-of-control behaviour, the
herb sending her crazy is causing no harm at all.

Pocket fact 🐾

About a third of all cats don't react to catnip at all. This is for genetic reasons: some cats simply don't have the genes which cause the crazy reaction.

CAT RECIPES

Cat cake

Ingredients: tuna, tinned cat food, dry cat food

Method:

- Mix equal ingredients of these three in a bowl (probably one you don't use to feed the kids with . . .).

- Compress the mixture into a baking tin, and scatter some more dry cat food on top, in a pretty pattern if you're creating a birthday cake.

- Place the concoction in the oven for a few minutes, check it isn't too hot, and serve it up in slices.

Tuna titbits

Ingredients: wholewheat flour, water, tuna, one egg

Method:

- Preheat the oven to 350°F, and cover some baking trays with greaseproof paper.

- Mash the tuna up until it's almost a paste, then gradually add the flour, along with a little water or cooking oil if you have some to hand. Once it's well mixed, beat the egg in a cup and gradually add this to the mixture; it should now be sticky and lumpy.

- Cover your hands in flour, and shape your dough into little cat-sized treats – make each one roughly the size of a marble. Once it's rolled, place it on the tray and flatten it with your thumb.

- Place in the oven for 10 minutes, then remove and turn each titbit over. Bake on the other side for about 10 minutes, then remove from the oven. Allow the titbits to cool completely before offering them to your cat. If they're a really special treat, add a little catnip as a finishing touch.

Feline feast

Ingredients: dry cat food, cream, water

Method:

- Put the cat food into a clear sandwich bag and then seal the top. With a heavy rolling pin, bash the cat food into little crumbs.

- Empty the bag of cat crumbs into a big bowl, then gradually add the water. Every minute or so, heat in the microwave, encouraging the mixture to form a paste.

- Once the water and crumbs have formed a thick paste (it shouldn't run at all but should be a fairly solid mixture), add a little cream (just enough to taste it), and mix. Serve with a little catnip if desired.

Pocket fact ❧

When cats walk or run they step with both left legs and then both right legs. Along with camels and giraffes they are the only animals in the world to walk in this way.

Cat Christmas cake

Ingredients: turkey, pumpkin, water, oil

Method:

- Prepare the turkey by mincing it – this can be done with a mincing machine. If you don't have one, don't worry; you can simply tear the turkey up into tiny pieces (until you're left with what's almost a turkey powder).

- Once it's done, mash the inside of half a pumpkin, carefully making sure that you've removed all the seeds.

- In a big bowl, mix the two together, adding a touch of oil to bind the mixture. Water can be added for extra binding, as the turkey will be dry and excess oil is bad for your cat and will cause their stools to become too wet.

- Once you've got a relatively firm mixture, compress it into a baking tin and warm it in the oven. Slice and sprinkle with catnip to serve.

OVERFEEDING AND OBESE CATS

The consequences of a cat being overweight are really serious. Your fat cat may look cute, but inside her little heart is beating too fast, her arteries are clogging up, and she's at real risk of a heart attack, amongst other illnesses. They tend to suffer from diabetes, hepatic lipidosis and arthritis due to all the strain on their joints caused by carrying extra and unnecessary weight.

As a rough guide, the average male cat should weigh between 9lbs and 12lbs, and the average female between 7lbs and 12lbs. You can usually tell if your cat is overweight without use of the scales, though: if your cat looks fat, it is.

Pocket fact ❧

Technically, if a cat is 20% over the average recommended body weight for their sex and body size, they are obese.

Just as in humans, there are two major causes for obesity in cats: diet and exercise.

- Diet, covered in the previous section, needs to be carefully regulated: not too much, not too little.

- Exercise is essential, and can be difficult to fit into the life of an indoor cat. If at all possible, try to let your cat outside every day – a quick run around will do it the world of good, and even older cats get excited when confronted with the great outdoors and all it has to offer. Chasing just one mouse a day significantly reduces the chances of your moggy becoming a fat cat.

Pocket fact ❧

Indoor cats are 57% more likely to be obese than outdoor cats.

What you can do
- Weigh your cat regularly to ensure that it isn't constantly gaining weight.

- If you think your cat is overweight, make a weight chart and keep track of her weight on a weekly basis.

- If you're unsure as to whether or not your cat needs help with dietary matters, check her weight with your vet.

- Get your cat exercising. If she has to stay indoors, buy or make some toys to encourage activity – things as simple as trailing a piece of string around the room can help. Instinct will force her to chase, and once she gets used to the idea of a bit of movement she'll enjoy it more and more.

- Look at her diet in detail. You don't have to feed her supermarket tinned food or dried food; there are always alternatives. Talk to your vet about putting her on a calorie-controlled diet; you can even buy diet cat food.

Pocket fact ❀

One in four cats in the UK is clinically obese – a disturbing figure. Think before you hand over those chicken scraps . . .

🐾 EQUIPMENT AND ACCESSORIES 🐾

Unlike many pets, your cat won't cost you too much, but you'll need a few basics.

CAT CARRIER

It is important to choose a good one, as you'll use it a lot throughout your cat's life, especially in the first year.

- There are many different types to consider: plastic and fibreglass, willow, metal.

- Make sure your carrier is the correct size for your cat. She should be able to stand up and move a little inside, and there should be room for her to stretch. However, make sure that it isn't too big: this may cause her to slide around on journeys and she will risk hurting herself. If you're not sure about sizes, check with your vet.

- Make sure your carrier is well ventilated and that your cat can see out of it. The fashionable 'cat bags' on the market really aren't ideal, because your pussycat will be traumatised inside. Stick with a sensible and solid carrier – she'll be much happier just knowing where she is.

FOOD BOWLS

Some people choose to feed their cats on a few old bowls and plates from their own kitchen. This is fine, as long as they're not big heavy china bowls that might hurt your cat if she puts her paw on the edge in excitement and hunger and knocks herself with it.

If you're buying your cat her own food bowls, consider:

- **Plastic bowls** may seem like an obvious choice, but they have a few downsides:

  o Firstly, many cats have an allergy to plastic, and cats can develop a skin condition on their chins that looks like acne and causes them discomfort.
  o The second disadvantage is that plastic isn't all that strong, so it tends to get scratches and little nicked bits in it that over time collect germs and cause bacteria to grow.
  o Plastic bowls are easy to clean and cheap to buy, but consider these disadvantages before you invest.

- **Stainless steel** bowls are a very popular option. They're generally quite a good choice to go with, as the material is strong and sturdy, and should last for a long time. The steel is also harmless to cats, safe and easy to pop in the dishwasher, and for these reasons stainless steel bowls tend to be the option strongly recommended by vets. They cost a little more than the plastic option, but should last forever and cause far fewer problems.

- **Ceramic bowls** also come strongly recommended by vets, but you must make absolutely sure that the glaze used on these is lead free, or your cat may be poisoned. Most are nowadays – it's just worth checking to be sure.

Whichever kind of bowls you decide upon, one of the most important things to remember is that you really need to keep them clean. Cats are very clean creatures, and will really turn their noses up at any of your carefully chosen food substances if you decide to present them in a grubby bowl, garnished with the remnants of yesterday's breakfast.

- If you feed your cats wet food, the bowls will need washing after every serving, as little leftover bits will dry up and become crusty within a few hours.

- If you serve your cat dry food, there's no need to wash the bowl every single day, but once every three days or so is highly recommended.

And if you forget, don't worry: your cat will soon let you know by refusing to touch her freshly served din-dins.

LITTER TRAYS

There are many different kinds on the market, and choosing one can be confusing. Cats are clean and private creatures, and in the wild they tend to do their business in areas that are as secluded and untouched as possible, quickly and tidily burying their waste immediately. Finding a way to mimic this environment in your home isn't the easiest thing in the world, but it can be done!

Basic litter tray rules

- Start with clean litter, and keep it clean.

- Buy litter that your cat will like to encourage use of the tray. Many different studies have shown that cats prefer to use clumping, scoopable litters. If your cat is coming from another home, find out what was used there as they don't tend to take too kindly to litter changes. If you're giving a kitten her first litter tray, try a few different options until she's happy to use it.

- Remember above all that every cat is different. One may want separate trays for stools and urine; one might not care. One might hate perfumed litter and the smell of cleaning products; another won't be fussed. Without pampering your cat excessively, just try to find out what she likes.

Pocket tip ✎

Try to have one litter tray for each cat if you have more than one, and perhaps one extra. This will mean they won't refuse to use a dirty litter tray.

Type of tray

- This should relate directly to the size of your cat: giving your little kitten a huge hooded litter tray that she can't even climb into obviously isn't a very sensible decision.

- A simple shallow rectangular tray with short sides is fine to start with: she'll be able to hop in and use it easily, and it's easy to clean and maintain. Once she starts growing bigger, or if you've got a bigger cat, there are other options to consider.

- You can opt for a big shallow tray: this is practical, and as long as you place it in a welcoming location your cat will be very satisfied.

- The other option is to buy a hooded tray. These look a bit like a cat carrier, and have detachable lids for cleaning. Your cat enters through a hole in the front, does her business, and exits. From your point of view these trays are quite wonderful: all mess is hidden away, and smells are confined. Cats might not like hooded trays though and might be put off by the smell that gets trapped inside, or feel restricted.

Location

- Keep trays away from food and water bowls, and try to place them in a quiet, private place.

- Cats will want their space, and this doesn't just mean time away from you and other animals, but also from noisy washing machines and hoovers. Try to do the best you can.

Pocket fact ❧

The Cheetah is the only cat in the world which can't retract its claws.

SCRATCHING POSTS

These can save your furniture – big time. Cats, especially those who don't spend very much time outdoors, need to keep their claws trimmed, and instinct tells them to scratch at every possible surface in order to do so.

- There's no need to get an expensive post; anything will do as long as it's big enough for her to have a good scratch and exercise her claws.

- Most are made of rope curled around a post.

- Rope isn't the only option, though. Some cats refuse to use rope scratching posts, but are more than happy to indulge in a good cardboardy scratch on a wound corrugated cardboard creation. These are becoming more and more popular; they often come as blocks or pyramids.

Pocket tip ❧

Sprinkling a bit of catnip on any scratching post makes it a temptation your cat won't be able to resist.

COLLARS

Get one – simple. Unless your cat is massively fat and it won't fit around her neck, she won't object at all, and indeed will probably be very happy if it manages to get her home from an overly ambitious adventure one day.

- It's probably best to use a flea collar for the added benefits.

- It's a good idea to get a personalised collar rather than a tag bearing your number, as tags can get lost and annoy cats. Don't put the cat's name on it: this tells strangers her name and they can instantly gain her trust and lure her somewhere untoward. Stick to phone number and address.

- Make sure it also has a quick-release buckle, in case your cat gets caught somewhere; this can prevent strangling and save her life.

Microchipping

This really is the most effective way of identifying a cat that gets lost. The microchip is smaller than a grain of rice and is quite painlessly injected between the cat's shoulder blades. When scanned by a vet or cattery, a number comes up which gives all details of the owner. It won't cost any more than £30, and should be less. Vets strongly recommend the procedure, and people whose cats have been returned after going missing understandably think it's the best invention since sliced bread.

TOYS

All cats love to play, and need to do so in order to stay fit and healthy. The world is a playground to your cat, and there's no need to spend a fortune on expensive and complicated playthings if you don't want to.

- Screw up a ball of paper – hours of energetic fun.

- Trail a piece of string or wool around your living room.

- Little plastic balls with bells inside can be bought for less than £1 yet provide hours and hours of fun and exercise for your cat. Best to buy more than one, though; your cat's crazy enthusiasm for chasing will probably mean it gets lost within a day of purchase.

If you do decide to splash out, there are some lovely creations available. Giant play centres and activity trees provide hours of fun, and can include scratching posts, cubby holes, balls on string, beds, and much more besides.

Pocket tip

Remember that not all cats take to these things, and many cats will be just as happy, if not happier, with a blanket thrown over an armchair and a ball of wool.

Popular cat toys

Here is a list of a few toys or items you can use to play with your beloved cat:

- torch or a laser pen

- ribbon on a stick

- catnip cigars

- a ball with a bell

- tickling feather.

And a few old favourites (or some cheaper alternatives):

- a ball of string

- a cardboard box

- a toy mouse

- paper.

And a few extravagances:

- a cat spa

- a deluxe cat tree

- a thermal cushion

- a doorbell for their cat flap.

CAT FLAPS

Cat flaps can be a real lifesaver, especially for the busy pussycat owner who leaves the house at 7am and isn't back until the same time in the evening. Having a little cat door means that she can come and go as she pleases, getting all the exercise she needs, staying fit and healthy, and even living longer.

- Some cat flaps are little doors fitted at the bottom of your own: they swing open and closed, and may have a little catch or lock so that you can shut them if you go away for a while (eg on holiday), or even if you just want to make sure she stays in at night.

- Electric cat flaps can have functions that let your cat in but not out, which is very useful when needing to take her to the vet. These work by attaching a little magnetic box to the collar.

- The fancier ones are even microchipped to make sure that only your cat can get in.

Cat flap problems exist but are pretty basic: just make sure your cat fits through the hole to start with, and make sure she knows how to use it and what it's for. You needn't worry too much about security issues as there's very little the average thief can do with a hole the size of his head – just make sure you close the latch if you're going to be away for a while, and keep an eye out for anything untoward.

Pocket fact ❧
Sir Isaac Newton invented the cat flap.

CAT BED

The three main types of bed available are basket, hooded basket and mat. Whichever you choose to buy, your cat will probably go and find her own bed anyway. Whatever happens, though, don't force your cat into the bought bed – she'll decide where she thinks is comfy, and as long as she's doing no harm, it's best to let her stay there.

🐈 BEHAVIOUR TRAINING 🐈

This isn't like dog training: your cat won't sit, stay or fetch. All your cat needs is a few pointers on how not to use plant pots as a litter tray, how not to tear the settee to shreds with her claws. She needs to know that the curtains aren't a huge climbing frame, and neither is your back.

From the day you bring your kitten home, certain rules need to be put in place and standards set: it's much fairer to her to set out boundaries from the beginning than to spoil her rotten for a month (as tempting as that may be), and then introduce rules.

- **Cats learn through experience.** If something pleasant happens to her, she will repeat whatever action caused it. If something bad happens, she probably won't go near whatever made it happen again, at least not after a few repeat experiences that have taught her it's not a good idea. This is the key to training: reward good behaviour, reprimand bad behaviour.

- **Try to understand what the cat is doing.** For example, if your cat is scratching the settee, she needs to sharpen her claws. You yelling at her really won't help – give her something to scratch that you don't mind being torn to shreds. Only once she's got this release for her needs do you have a right to punish, and even then you need to be careful.

- **Punishment should never be physical.** Instead, try some of the following, and remember that you want her to associate unpleasantness with the naughty act, and not with you:

  o Have a water squirter to hand, and give her a quick squirt if you catch her doing something naughty. It won't hurt and it's not you that's causing the unpleasantness, but she won't like it. Try to do it every time she misbehaves, and she will soon learn that settee scratching equals getting wet, and stop.

○ You can have the same effect with a few other objects and ideas:

- a can of compressed air
- a cap gun
- a hand-held alarm
- a simple 'hiss' – this is cat language for 'no!', or 'stop it!', or 'I don't like it!' – simple, but effective.

Pocket tip 🧶

Cats are clever, and to outwit them you need to be clever too. Never be cruel, just try to be fair.

- **'Remote punishment'** means punishing naughty behaviour even when you can't do it yourself. This will stop your cat misbehaving when you're out. It's a good idea to administer punishment from a distance even when you're there – perhaps hide around a corner while you spray your cat. This way the association between act and consequence is reinforced. Then, when you're not there the cat will expect the punishment anyway.

- **Make areas where your cat is prone to misbehave undesirable for her.**

○ Drape a piece of loose material over a chair she likes to scratch, making the experience unappealing, as loose fabric can't really be clawed like a nice tight settee can.

o Try tricks like balancing a stack of tin cans on the arm of a chair she scratches, so that they fall on her if she tries to do it (make sure they're empty and have no serrated edges – you want to shock her, not hurt her!)

o Put double-sided tape on the arms of chairs – this will definitely take the fun and satisfaction out of the act.

It's just as important to praise good behaviour as it is to punish your cat when she misbehaves. Every time she uses her litter tray correctly or sleeps in her cat bed, give her plenty of fuss (provided she wants it, of course), and reward her with titbits (small ones, or she'll get fat). Kittens won't react to catnip because they aren't sexually mature, but once they hit the right age you can use this as a treat too, along with plenty of love and playtime.

Pocket tip

Don't forget that recurring problems may be behavioural and indicate that there is something more wrong than your cat being a bit naughty.

What to do if your cat attacks furniture

Don't get angry with your moggy if she decides that your new three-piece suite looks like an excellent option: she's only doing what nature tells her to. Buy her a scratching post, and place her next to it at regular intervals until she gets used to the idea that she will be rewarded for scratching here (but gently reprimanded for tearing the furniture to pieces).

If she's got a post, but still scratches where she shouldn't, take a look at the ideas above.

🐈 POTENTIAL OWNERSHIP 🐈 PROBLEMS

Owning a cat isn't all about fluffy kitty tales – there are a few responsibilities you need to take into consideration too.

PONDS

Be careful if you have a pond outside. Cats are born fishermen and will almost certainly try to kill anything you have in the pond. It's especially important to bear this in mind if your neighbours have ponds, or pet birds. It really is your responsibility to make sure she doesn't misbehave and slip under the fence to practise her hunting skills. Ask your neighbour if there's any possibility they can cover their pond, and keep an eye on your cat's activities.

Pocket tip 🧶

It's important to co-operate with neighbours where your pets are concerned: remember, if your cat goes missing one day you may really need their help.

HUNTING CATS

Cats who hunt can cause real problems, both for you and those around you. Catching mice and rats is unlikely to really upset anyone, unless they are pets. If it happens too frequently it can become a problem. In the countryside, there can be bigger problems than mice and birds on the doorstep. Both rabbits and chickens can be targets for the adventurous moggy.

Pocket fact ❧

Evidence suggests that the cats found on the Kenyan islands in the Lamu Archipelago are the direct descendants of the sacred cats worshipped in ancient Egypt.

There is relatively little you can do with your cat other than keep her indoors (which will do her no good, and is quite a big compromise).

One option is to invest in a cat bib – this is a little neoprene triangle that attaches to their collar and prevents them from being agile enough to catch prey.

If it's affecting your neighbours, talk to them. Is the pond or rabbit area fenced off properly? If not, suggest it: this will protect against all predators, not just your cat.

Cats catch more birds during the summer season and, contrary to popular belief, they are just as likely to hunt after being fed as they are when they're hungry. Hunting is down to instinct, not hunger.

Pocket fact ❧

Cats and chickens often get along. In 2007, a story was reported of a Japanese cat who took seven chicks under her wing and cared for them after their mother died. They lived in harmony with her four newborn kittens and together made a very happy, if extraordinary, fluffy family.

GARDENERS THAT HATE CATS

The other main problem with keeping cats comes from complaints from gardeners: a flowerbed is a litter tray, a big game full of colourful toys. To some gardeners, your cat is a pesky little beast that spoils hours of hard work and leaves little brown piles where blooming buds of flowers should be.

- Most gardeners resort to squirting the cat with water whenever she approaches flowerbeds, but this isn't always practical for those who work.

- To ensure round-the-clock protection for gardens, you can suggest an ultrasonic deterrent that emits sounds that are unpleasant to your cat's ears. These cost about £25, and it may even be worth investing in one for your neighbour if you can afford it: it could be worth it to keep the peace.

Pocket fact ❧

Bus drivers in the West Midlands have an unexpected passenger: since January 2007, a white haired cat with different colour eyes gets on the number 331 bus two or three times a week. He gets on and off at the same stops each day, only travelling 400m. The bus drivers have named him Macavity, and no one knows who his owners are.

Pocket fact ❧

A Califonrnian Spangled Cat was bought for $24,000 (£15,925) in January 1987 and was the display cat from the Neiman Marcus Christmas Book of 1986

Cat tricks

Cats are intelligent animals and it is possible to teach them tricks. There are even some people who claim they have taught their cat to use the toilet! Like dogs, cats can be taught to sit, come and even shake hands (or paws).

If you want to shake hands with your cat, try using food rewards to teach your cat tricks, as they most often respond to positive reinforcement. However, most cat owners will argue that until a cat decides on their own to learn a trick, they will refuse to learn it!

If you really want to teach them a trick, try to work on something they already do naturally as a behaviour (like jumping when the doorbell rings). And be patient; it won't happen right away!

🐾 COMMUNICATION 🐾

'I can say with sincerity that I like cats. A cat is an animal which has more human feeling than almost any other.'
Emily Brontë

Cats communicate in a more complex way than you might imagine: they're not restricted to just purring and meowing. In order to convey things to other cats, they often use body language, and noises help with this. They also bite, scratch, purr, tap . . .

Pocket fact 🐾
When your cat rubs against your legs, it isn't just showing affection; it is marking you with its scent.

BODY LANGUAGE

Some of the signs cats exhibit are easily interpreted and make a lot of sense; others aren't and don't.

Back arching

Pretty obvious. Your cat is trying to look as big and scary as possible to ward off potential attackers. For such small creatures, cats can succeed in looking really quite scary.

Sprawling

This usually signifies submission, trust and affection. It's also associated with relaxation, and your cat may languidly roll over and show you her tummy to show love when you enter the room, or even if you just stir in your chair.

Shaking/lifting of paws

Shaking of paws and acting as though she's standing in a puddle usually means your cat is probably disgusted. The more paws she lifts and shakes, the more disgusted she is.

Pocket fact ❧

A cat's brain has more similarities with a human brain than that of a dog. In both humans and cats the same region in the brain is responsible for emotion.

Pawing/kneading

If your cat does this to you, she's very happy and loves you. She probably won't do this for more than 10 minutes at a time, but is actually simulating the action she used to get milk out of her mother when she was a kitten. This shows that she is utterly relaxed.

Swishing her tail

This probably means that your cat is trying to show aggression. It could also mean that she wants to get your attention for some reason.

Head rubbing

When your cat presses her head and body against you it's her way of showing affection. She's also marking you, though, using her scent to make you 'hers'.

BITING

This isn't just pointless aggression. Different bites can mean different things, and it's actually quite rare for a cat to bite aggressively, especially without reason.

Nipping

This is affectionate and painless. Your cat may nip you if she is feeling calm and contented, and she'll often accompany the action with purring, head rubbing, and an upright stiff tail. Nipping can barely be felt, and is the weakest and friendliest form of biting.

Playful biting

This is often accompanied by clawing, and you can usually tell that your cat is playing by her movements and excitement. She may bite toys she is playing with, or mistake your fingers for a toy and bite them too. Kittens are especially likely to do this, and often they have no idea that they possess the ability to injure others.

Pocket tip

Playful biting can hurt a little, but isn't malicious and you should just remove your hand rather than punishing your cat.

'Polite request' biting

This borders on aggressive and painful, but it isn't really either. If you're stroking your cat, for example, and she's enjoyed it but eventually has enough and wants to go to sleep, she has to let you know somehow. The easiest way for her to do that is to bite whatever is annoying her: it will inevitably stop as a result.

There will be other signs that she's annoyed, too, and you can get the message before she resorts to biting if you manage to notice that she's stopped purring, her tail is swishing, and her ears may be pointing backwards. Just stop whatever you're doing and walk away.

Aggressive biting

This is intended to hurt, and will do so. Cats don't bite aggressively very often, but if provoked or upset they will defend themselves with their teeth, and can do quite some damage. Cats especially prone to this include those who are injured, and mothers protecting their kittens. Biting should be reprimanded – if your cat bites you aggressively, ignore her for about 15 minutes and make it clear you're upset by making a noise that suggests you're in pain.

PURRING

Everybody knows that cats purr when they're happy, but not many people are aware that purring doesn't always equal contentedness. Obviously, if they're really happy this is how they'll express it, but cats also purr if they're feeling unwell or if something has upset them. It has also been recorded that some cats even purr when they know they're dying.

Pocket fact ❧

Cats that live in the wild are much quieter than their domesticated counterparts. This is because cats learn that humans respond to vocal communication, but it isn't necessary to converse with other animals.

NOISES

A meow may be the most obvious cat noise, but they make quite a few, and most can be interpreted quite easily. Meowing can happen in different tones and mean different things, but it's mostly directed at humans and cats tend to communicate with other cats in different ways. You can usually guess from the kind of meow what your cat wants, and you'll also get to know in time what she means – it's pretty obvious that if she's sitting by the back door yowling, she probably wants to be let out.

Pocket fact ❧

French researchers claim that the domestic cat has a vocal range of as many as 60 notes. These go from soft purring to growling and, at the other end of the scale, howling.

When communicating with other cats, there are lots of other noises you might overhear and not quite understand.

Growling and hissing

Unsurprisingly, these aren't happy sounds, and if you overhear your cat doing either it's usually a warning that the cat is angry, and if the recipient doesn't take note of this warning a fight will probably break out. If your cat is growling and hissing, it may well soon be scratching and biting.

Pocket fact ❧

A cat's cry is called a caterwaul.

Snorting

This usually indicates frustration, for example if your cat has tried to catch some prey but failed at the last minute. It's just a sign of annoyance, and happens when they exhale suddenly.

Chattering and chirping

This happens when cats are stalking prey and can sound really strange. Nobody really knows whether it's supposed to be frightening and threatening, or just an excited sound that cats can't help. It has also been suggested that the sound is meant to mimic bird noises and attract them; this is possible, but scientists have noted that the sound occurs at the moment when cats bite the neck of their prey in a killing movement and so it is probably in anticipation of this.

Humming sounds

When your cat is asleep, she may make soft, contented humming sounds. This often happens if you stroke her when she's asleep, or may mean that she's dreaming, especially if her paws are twitching.

Can cats talk?

Sound crazy? There have, however, been numerous scientific surveys carried out on the topic. Mildred Moelk, in 1944, succeeded in dividing the sounds made by cats into the following three groups:

- *open-mouthed sounds*
- *closed-mouth murmuring sounds*
- *closed-mouth vowel sounds*

According to Mildred's study, cats make 16 different sounds, all of which can be translated to acquire human meaning. Whether or not this is true is questionable, but most cat owners are more than capable of interpreting the little noises made by their cats, and there is no mistaking the hungry yowling for food or desperate pleas to be let out to play.

🐾 DIFFERENT PERSONALITIES 🐾

What makes your cat so special is that she is unique. The differences between each individual cat basically come down to the old nature vs. nurture argument. Some traits are down to genetic make-up, whilst others are determined by upbringing and environment.

The most important stage of this in cats occurs during the 'social-isation' period, which usually takes place between the ages of two and eight weeks and is the time when the kitten builds up her picture of the human race and the world around her. Much of her personality is shaped during this period.

Pocket tip 🧶

If your cat doesn't encounter any men (or doesn't live with one at least) for these first few weeks, then she may well grow up to be frightened of them, associating his male voice and bigger build with another, unfamiliar species.

There are three 'types' of personality in cats.

- **Equable:** This can basically mean two things. Your cat may either be rather stoic and complacent, as a result of having sur-vived traumatic incidents in the past (common in rescue cats), or she may fly off the handle without any apparent reason due to the same kind of traumatic past.

- **Sociable:** The sociable cat wants to be with you, chat to you, play with you . . . perfect if you like cats who have a real pres-ence in the house. They don't have any great fear of humans or other cats, and aren't a great worry to their owners.

- **Alert:** Cats who are alert can be either equable or sociable, but they needn't necessarily be either. If they are classified as alert, it means that they are naturally curious and inquisitive. This usually refers to a cat that has her nose in everything, wants to discover the world around her and is fascinated by every movement and sound in her environment.

Temperament obviously varies between cats, but can at least be guessed to a certain extent where specific breeds are concerned (see the section 'Breeds of Pedigree Cat' starting on p. 25). Moggies can't be second-guessed and every cat varies – some hate being indoors, others never want to venture past the doorstep; some crave your cuddles, others prefer to lounge in solitude amongst your clean laundry.

Fragile and shy scaredy-cats can actually be quite difficult to deal with. They aren't uncommon, especially if they've had a challenging first few weeks of life. A soft, gentle approach and peaceful environment are the best things you can provide for such a moggy.

What do cats do all day?

You immediately think 'not much'. And you wouldn't be far wrong. Cats are renowned for their lazy nap-loving attitude to life, and their luxurious lifestyle is envied by almost every hardworking human alive.

A cat sleeps over twice as much as we do: they spend two-thirds of their life asleep. That's 13–16 hours a day in bed.

🐈 PREGNANT CATS 🐈

HOW CAN YOU TELL WHEN YOUR CAT IS PREGNANT?

There are a few signs you should look out for, especially if a stray has plonked herself on your doorstep and is begging for love and attention. If your cat hasn't been spayed, get it done. In the meantime, keep your eye out for the following signs:

Pocket fact 🐾
Cats are pregnant for nine weeks before giving birth, or anytime from 60–67 days.
During her life a female cat can have more than 100 kittens.

Personality changes

Increased affection
This is especially noticeable in cats that are usually quite solitary and independent. If your cat suddenly starts craving attention, ask yourself why.

Nesting activities
Whereas humans may get instinctive desires to clean and tidy in preparation for their new arrival, cats devote their time to seeking out a place for the birth. If you notice your cat nosing around quiet, secluded places she might be about to have kittens, but unless she's generally fat you will probably have noticed that she's pregnant by this stage anyway.

Decreased activity
If your cat usually tears around the house at breakneck speed, but has now suddenly taken to moving a little more slowly and reclining by the fire, something has probably changed.

Physical changes

Increased appetite
Like humans, cats may suddenly find themselves very hungry. This isn't surprising, given that whereas humans claim to be 'eating for two', cats are probably eating for four or five!

Vomiting
Your cat may suffer 'morning sickness', as despite being a feline her body is experiencing many of the same changes as a human female. Don't worry about a bit of vomiting, but if it gets really regular or she seems to be throwing up everything she eats, it's probably best to call the vet.

Heat cycles stop
Females who haven't been spayed will have a heat cycle every 10 days or so. These are really quite evident (see below), and you will almost certainly notice if they suddenly disappear – take this as a sign she is almost certainly pregnant.

Nipple swelling
This is the first visible physical sign, and is commonly known as 'pinking' amongst breeders. It may not sound that obvious, but the nipples really do become so swollen that you can't help but notice whenever your cat rolls onto her back.

Fat tummy
The most obvious sign of pregnancy in all mammals! This will start to show about five weeks into the pregnancy.

Pocket fact ❧

Heat cycles occur every 10–14 days in cats. They can be recognised by her licking her genitals, practising mating positions (head down, rear end raised), spraying surfaces with a strong-smelling fluid and, most obviously, yowling loudly. This behaviour will continue until she is spayed or gets pregnant.

My cat is pregnant – what do I do?

Take your cat to the vet if you suspect that she might be pregnant, but admittedly sometimes it can be so obvious that there's no need. An advantage of making the trip is that your vet can check everything is in order and that your cat and her kittens are all healthy. The vet trip is essential if you've decided to take in a pregnant stray, as she needs to be checked for diseases that could be passed on to any other cats you may have.

Cat pregnancy has three stages:

1. **First Trimester:** Organic structures are formed and the embryo becomes the foetus.

2. **Second Trimester:** Development of foetus.

3. **Third Trimester:** Growth of foetus into kitten ready to be born.

During all this time, your cat needs a good, nutritious diet and plenty of fresh clean water. Try to feed her small, regular meals rather than large ones: her tummy is full of kittens and she doesn't have enough space to eat vast quantities of food.

Labour and birth

This should be a process that doesn't require your help. Cats are usually capable of giving birth unassisted, so just keep an eye from a distance and don't interfere unless things really seem to be going wrong. But how do you know what is normal?

Watch out for the signs of early labour. These include restlessness, pacing and searching for a place to give birth. She will become very vocal and make trips to the litter tray without passing stools or urine. Eventually, she will settle down into her chosen maternity bed (whether this has been provided by you or is a spot she has chosen herself, either is fine).

The labour will begin and your cat may scream when her first kitten is born. The labour can last up to 12 hours and kittens may emerge either head or feet first: both are fine. Gaps between births can range between 30 minutes to an hour.

You should only become concerned if you see her straining hard and excessively without a kitten being born. Excessive bloody discharge is also cause for concern, and a vet should be called. Don't move your cat when she is in labour.

Once the kitten is born, your cat should break the amniotic fluid around it. If she doesn't, this is where you should intervene – use a towel and gently break the sac. Never ever use a knife; you could seriously injure the kitten.

Your cat should then clean the kitten, getting rid of membranes and stimulating breathing. If this doesn't happen, do it yourself with a towel: it's necessary to get the breathing going.

The last point you may need to intervene on is the cutting of the umbilical cord. Again, your cat should bite it and all should be fine, but if she doesn't then you should tie some dental floss around the cord about an inch from the kitten's body, and cut the cord on the mother's side of the tie. If you cut it too close, you could injure or even kill the kitten, so be careful and if you think your cat is getting too close, stop her.

Delivery usually takes around 5 hours, but can last about 12. If your cat seems to be having difficulty giving birth, rubbing petroleum jelly on her can really help. All in all, it should be a relatively simple process that you shouldn't have to intervene in.

Pocket fact ❖

Cats have an average of two to five kittens, but a litter can consist of anything between one and eight.

❧ SEASONAL CONSIDERATIONS ❧

Your cat will be affected by celebrations and seasonal festivities. Sometimes they can upset her, sometimes she loves it. Christmas turkey will usually go down a treat, but bangs on Bonfire Night might not.

- **New Year:** This really is a night for her to stay indoors – most of the country will be staggering around drunk, driving around drunk, letting off fireworks and making loud banging noises . . . drunk. It's not safe for her to be out in the midst of all of this. The risk of her being hurt or run over is significantly increased: just shut her in safely.

- **Easter:** Keep chocolate eggs hidden; they won't do your cat any good.

- **Summer holidays:** Having neighbours around twice a day to feed your cat is usually the best option when you go away. The other option is to send your cat to a cattery.

- **Halloween:** It's probably best to keep your cat locked inside just in case: even though she probably won't be scared of any costumes, screaming and excitable children could scare her.

- **Bonfire Night:** Probably the most frightening night of the year for your cat, along with New Year. The fireworks really can be terrifying, and many cats are known to run away on 5 November; many get locked in sheds in their attempts to hide, and go permanently missing. There is one solution: keep your cat safely locked inside where she can hide under the settee.

- **Christmas** is heaven for some cats; what could be better than an ocean of wrapping paper to pounce on, a crazy tree to climb, the smell of turkey in the air, and a never-ending supply of ornaments to bat about the floor to your heart's content? There are a few things you need to consider, though. If you're having visitors your cat may get scared – give her a quiet space where she can hide. Try not to let her eat too much and become unwell. And again, beware of all the chocolate around.

Pocket fact 🐾

The longest cat in the world is Leo (full name Leonetti). He is as long as an 8-year-old child and has paws so big they can fit into a child's shoe! If Leo stood upright, he would stretch over 2.5 m (8 feet) tall.

Leo is a Maine Coon cat – normally a large breed, Maine Coons often weigh as much as 10 kg (22 lb), but Leo weighs in at a whopping 15.8 kg (35 lb) and measures a record-breaking 121.9 cm (48 in) from nose to tail.

Catteries

If you are going away on holiday make sure you plan where your cat is going to stay well in advance as catteries can book up very quickly. You can ask your vet or other cat owners for recommendations. Make sure you phone as many catteries as possible to be sure you find one you are happy with.

Make an appointment to visit the cattery before you send your cat there. Ask the owner about essential things like the exercise your cat will receive, how they will be fed (can you use your own food?), and where your cat will sleep. Make sure you check out the living quarters to ensure they are clean and spacious with separate sleeping quarters. Some catteries have an outdoor area, while others only have indoor facilities. You should choose based on the type of lifestyle your cat enjoys at home.

The cattery will probably ask you about any vaccinations your cat has received and if they have been in contact with other animals. You will probably have to provide vaccination certificates before they will accept your cat. Most catteries will also ask you to provide your own bedding for your cat. Having their own blanket or cushion can be comforting for your cat while they are in a strange location. You can also give them their favourite toy.

Before you send your cat to a cattery, make sure you tell the cattery about any medications your cat is taking and ask what they would do if your cat fell ill. If your cat is on a special diet, also make sure they are aware of this. Make sure you give the cattery a contact telephone number as well as the contact details of your vet.

❧ CATS AND THE LAW ❧

- The Animal Welfare Act was introduced in 2007. This not only states that animal cruelty is illegal, but also sets out requirements for the proper care of all animals. Legal duties when caring for an animal include ensuring that they have a clean and suitable environment, good diet and are protected from pain, suffering and disease. Failure to provide any of these things can result in jail and a fine of £20,000.

- Cats are also covered under the Theft Act of 1968. They are considered the 'property' of their owner, and stealing a cat is treated in exactly the same way as theft of any other object or belonging.

- The Criminal Damage Act 1971 also applies to cats. This means that because the law regards cats as property, an offence may be committed under this Act if anybody kills or injures a cat belonging to somebody else without lawful excuse.

- Unlike dogs, cats are basically allowed to roam wherever they like: the law recognises that this is in their nature and they can't be controlled like their canine counterparts. They are also less likely to cause damage to people and property than other animals. There is, however, a general duty of law to take reasonable care to ensure that cats do not injure people, animals or property. Cases of this nature are rarely taken to court, but try to make sure that your cat isn't spending seven days a week terrorising the chickens on the farm next door.

- Planning and environmental law states that if large numbers of cats are kept at a domestic residence, the owner may be required to make a planning application for change of use of the property. If too many cats are kept in a property, the Environmental Protection Act 1990 can be used by the Environmental Health Department, for example if there is excess yowling or fouling. Lesson: don't become the old lady with hundreds of cats, because the law will win.

• Cats can travel between countries under PETS (Pet Travel Scheme).

Pocket fact ❧

In March 2006, Lewis, a cat from Fairfield, Connecticut, was put under house arrest. Serveral of the town's residents had accused Lewis of attacking them, without provocation. His owner, Ruth Cisero, was also arrested, but refused bail (on the condition that Lewis had to be put down). Cisero was tried, and received two years' probation. Lewis escaped death, but is only allowed out of the house to visit the vet in a cage.

TIPS ON OWNING A CAT

- Carefully consider the cost (such as food and insurance fees) and long term commitment (some cats can live for up to 20 years) that go along with owning a cat.
- Make sure your lifestyle will suit owning a cat: do you have the time to groom a longhaired cat and are you prepared to make important decisions such as declawing or neutering?
- You will also have to consider if you want a cat or a kitten, a pedigree or a moggy, a male or a female.
- Be careful when choosing where you get your cat from: make sure you check the health of a cat from a cattery or a stray that you adopt.
- Make sure you have all the essentials before your new cat arrives home, such as food and water bowls, a litter tray and litter, toys, a bed, a scratching post, a brush and an ID collar.
- Make sure your cat has its own area for its litter tray, and a separate place for her food and water bowls far away from this.
- Make sure you handle your kitten often so they will be used to human contact and wont become nervous around people.
- Reward good behaviour from your kitten and if she misbehaves tell her off in a firm voice and ignore her, she'll soon learn what's acceptable.
- You will need to decide if you want to have your cat spayed or neutered and if you want to have her microchipped.

- Make sure you know how to care for your cat at different stages of its life.
- Monitor your cat's health and keep an eye out for signs of common illness or infection.
- Know what type of coat your cat has and how to groom it. Make sure you keep up essential maintenance such as claw clipping.
- Know the different types of cat food available and when you should give them to your cat.
- Learn to understand your cat's behaviour, body language and meows so you know what they are trying to tell you and how to deal with it.
- Know how to look after your cat's needs during the different seasons.
- Make cattery or travel arrangements (such as a pet passport) well in advance.
- Have fun with your cat. Cats are wonderful companions: make sure you enjoy owning one!

USEFUL TERMINOLOGY

Agouti: the colour between the stripes of a tabby cat.

Ailurophile: a person who loves cats.

Ailurophobe: a person who is afraid of cats.

Awn hairs: the secondary hairs on a cat's coat which are bristly with thick tips.

Banding: bands of colour which grow individually in a cross-wise direction.

Bib: part of the ruff, this is the longer hair around a cat's chest.

Blaze: markings which runs down the centre of a cat's forehead, nose and chin.

Blue: coat colour which appears blue or grey.

Boar cat: an older term for a tom cat or an unneutered male cat.

Bracelets: darker stripes on the legs of tabby cats.

Break: a change in the direction of the profile of the nose. Common in Persian breeds.

Calico: tri-coloured coat pattern of a white background with black, brown and orange.

Calling: the behaviour of a female cat during heat, particularly yelling and howling.

Cameo-Chincilla: shaded coat with red or cream tipping.

Carpal pads: the pads on a cat's front legs which give traction while walking.

Catnip: a herb which produces a strong reaction in some cats, but not in all cats.

Cattery: a place to leave your cat while you go away or to adopt your cat from.

Chincilla: a white or pale coat where only the outer tips are black or another colour.

Clowder: a group of cats.

Cornish Rex: a cat with no hair except for the undercoat.

Dam: a female parent cat.

Down hairs: the short, soft secondary hairs.

Elizabethan collar: a plastic or card collar which goes round a cat's neck to prevent it from licking a wound and allow it to heal.

Fading kittens: kittens which die despite appearing to be healthy at birth. Normally thought to be as a result of poor nutrition, infection or abnormalities.

Feral: a wild cat which has not been socialised.

Free-feed: allowing a cat unlimited access to its food bowl.

Ghost markings: faint tabby markings on solid coloured cats.

Gib: a neutered tomcat.

Guard hair: long, coarse hairs which make up the outer coat.

Hairball: balls of hair which collect in the stomach after grooming and are expelled by vomiting.

Heat: the period in which a female cat is in her breeding season.

Hock: the ankle of a cat's hind leg.

Home range: the inner area of a cat's territory.

Hunting range: the area of a cat's territory where it will hunt but not sleep.

Jacobsen's Organ: an organ located in a cat's mouth which acts as both a smell and a taste organ.

Laces: the white markings on a cat's legs.

Litter: a group of kittens born at one time.

Locket: a solid white marking on a cat's neck.

Mask: the darker markings on a cat's face, particularly in Siamese and Himalayan cats.

Moggy: a mixed breed cat.

Moult: when a cat sheds its hair periodically.

Mitted: white marks on a cat's paws.

Necklace: bands of colour across the chest and lower neck.

Nose pad: hard skin around a cat's nostrils.

Pedigree: cat with an established lineage.

Piebald: coat with patches of two colours, normally black and white.

Pica: condition where cat eats inedible items such as wool or material.

Pinnae: flaps of the ear.

Pointed: coat pattern of a solid body colour with darker colour on the face, ears, legs and tail.

Points: extreme points of a cat's body, such as the ears and tail.

Polydactyl: extra toes on the feet.

Pricked: ears held apart.

Queen: an adult female.

Red: a coat colour, also called orange, marmalade or ginger.

Righting reflex: the ability cat's have of righting themselves while falling.

Ruff: long, thick hair around the neck and chest.

Secondary coat: fine hairs which the undercoat is made of.

Shading: gradual change in coat colour, normally from back to stomach.

Sire: a male parent cat.

Socialisation: kittens should be socialised between two and eight weeks to familiarise themselves with people and their environment.

Spay/neuter: removal of reproductive organs.

Spotting: white patches on the coat.

Tabby: coat pattern of stripes, dots or swirls.

Tapeturn Lucidum: layer of tissue behind the retina which helps the cat's vision at night.

Territory: area in which a cat lives and feeds. Cats will defend their territory from other cats and it can be a common cause of behavioural problems.

Ticking: coat with black flecks.

Tipped: the coloured ends of a cat's hair.

Tomcat: a male cat.

Tortoiseshell: coat pattern of orange and brown.

Undercoat: section of a cat's coat made up of down hairs.

Undercolour: colour of the hair closest to the cat's skin.

Van pattern: coat which has a white body with colour only at the extremities, for example the tail and head.

Vestibular apparatus: an organ in the inner ear which helps cats with their righting reflex to land on their feet.

Vibrissae: technical term for a cat's whiskers.

Whisker pad: thick, fatty pads around a cat's whiskers.

USEFUL CONTACTS

All About Pets
Pet care information service provided by The Blue Cross, with a pet forum community.
www.allaboutpets.org.uk

Animal Care
An informative site for pet owners, with advice on animal care.
www.animal-care.co.uk

Animal Search UK
A free advertising/listing service for your lost or found pet.
01432 761 406
info@animalsearchuk.com
www.animalsearchuk.com

Animals in Mind
A UK charity specialising in pet behaviour.
www.animalsinmind.org.uk

Battersea Dogs & Cats Home
A good place to look for cats to adopt as pets.
www.battersea.org.uk

Cat Chat
A web-based charity, with a 'Virtual Cat Shelter' search engine. Also has a community forum.
www.catchat.org

Cat Knowledge Base (Cat KB)
A community for cat lovers with a comprehensive discussion forum.
www.CatKB.com

Cats International
Advice on a variety of feline behaviour problems.
www.catsinternational.org

Cats Protection
Re-homes and reunites 55,000 cats per year. A range of leaflets are available on all aspects of cat care.
08702 099099 (National Helpline)
08707 708 650 (Adoption Centre)
helpline@cats.org.uk
www.cats.org.uk

Felipedia
A reference site for feline diseases.
www.felipedia.org

The Feline Advisory Bureau
A charity dedicated to promoting the health and welfare of cats. Information sheets on a range of feline conditions are available via their web site. The site also contains a nationwide list of FAB approved catteries.
0870 742 2278
information@fabcats.org
www.fabcats.org

Missing Pets Bureau

Operates a national Missing Pets Register and works closely with 12,000 pet care organisations.

www.petsbureau.co.uk

National Animal Welfare Trust

An independent charity that runs rescue and re-homing centres throughout the UK, in Berkshire, Cornwall, Somerset, Essex and London and the Home Counties.

www.nawt.org.uk

020 8950 0177

National Cat Club

Has run an annual show since 1887.

www.nationalcatclub.co.uk

PDSA

Cares for the pets of needy people by providing free veterinary services.

0800 731 2502

www.pdsa.org.uk

PetsAndTravel

Information on travelling with your pet. There is an 'Ask Our Experts' forum on the website.

www.petsandtravel.co.uk

Pet Health Care

Provides professional advice on a wide range of cat health issues. Includes the 'Well Cat Clinic', special care for senior cats, how to give a tablet, a vets directory and lots more

www.pethealthcare.co.uk

The Society of Feline Artists

Founded in September 1994, promotes the work of the cat artists, whether established or unknown. They have had an annual exhibition of cat paintings in London, featuring over 100 artists.

www.felineartists.org

VetInfo

A comprehensive health information service for cats. Includes an 'Ask a Vet Online' enquiry service

www.vetinfo.com

Your Cat Magazine

Magazine for caring cat owners, covering health and behaviour, general care advice, breed information, and other practical issues.

www.yourcat.co.uk

INDEX

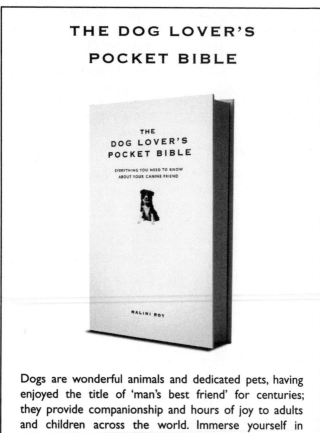